HANDS ON!

Science Activities

for K-3

Christine Economos

Troll Associates

Interior Illustrations by: Shirley Beckes

ISBN: 0-8167-2591-8

Printed in the United States of America.

10 9 8 7 6 5 4 3 2

Contents

THE WEATHER

MATTER

MOTION

ENERGY

Introduction

Welcome to the wonderful world of science! At this point in their lives young children are learning about their environment and their world. They are curious, imaginative, and inquisitive. *Hands-On Science Activities: K–3* will open their eyes to the great big wondrous magic show of science. The activities in this book are geared to encouraging students to explore, inspect, watch, and examine the world around them.

Preparing for Activities

The science activities are designed to give your students hands-on experience with science concepts and processes. To help students get the most from the activities, review the activity and collect the necessary materials ahead of time. Most of the materials can be found at home or in the school. Occasionally you will need to get materials from a hardware store or supermarket. For science materials pertaining to biology that may be difficult to find, you may wish to contact the Carolina Biological Supply Company at (919) 584-0381. Prepare student activity sheets or introductory materials to be used. Set up activity tables to accommodate small groups of students.

The ''Plan'' section of each activity provides an introduction that motivates students and provides focus. Encourage students to develop their own understanding of concepts and terms by discussing with them related ideas and any questions. As you present the science question they will be investigating, be sure to explain any necessary safety rules.

Cooperative-Learning Groups

The use of small learning groups will give students the opportunity to benefit from cooperative peer interaction. Try to balance the groups in terms of students' abilities and personalities. You may want to give each group member a particular task within the scope of the activity: a task supervisor could be in charge of supervising the activity; a supply manager could be in charge of gathering the supplies the group needs; a reporter could record the group's observations and findings and report to the rest of the class;

a cleanup supervisor could make sure the group cleans up and returns materials to their proper place. You may want to change the composition of the groups with each activity to allow students to fulfill different roles and to encourage new working relationships among peers.

Getting Started

Have supply managers collect materials and return to their groups to begin an activity. Set a time limit and let students know when only ten minutes remain so that they can begin to finish the task. As students work, move around among the groups to ask questions, stimulate thinking, help students refocus their attention, encourage students to participate, and help to keep groups on task. When the activities are completed, ask cleanup supervisors to make sure groups return the materials. Then conduct a class discussion, allowing group reporters time to share their groups' findings and observations.

Most of the activities can be done any time of year. However, some times are better than others for trying out some activities in this book. Activities involving plants and their growth are best done in early fall or late spring. Cold-weather activities should be done in the winter.

What Are the Parts of Plants?

Concept: All plants have roots, stems, and leaves.

Materials: Fresh vegetables with roots and leaves still attached, such as carrots, celery, beets, scallions; a small houseplant; activity sheet for each student (page 8).

Plan: Display the houseplant and ask students to name its parts, writing their responses on the chalkboard. You may want to make a diagram like the one below.

Tell students that all plants have roots, stems, and leaves and that these parts may look different on different plants. Remind students that many plants also have flowers and fruit.

Have students work in groups. Give each group one of the vegetables and ask them to identify the roots, stems, and leaves. You may want one student in each group to record the group's findings by illustrating and labeling the parts. Have groups exchange vegetables so that all have an opportunity to identify the parts of each vegetable. Allow groups time to share their observations.

Take students on a walk to a local park and have them observe the various plants. Help younger students identify the roots, stems, and leaves, as well as any flowers and fruit, of trees, shrubs, flowers, and other plants. Have older students illustrate three different kinds of plants on their activity sheets, reminding them to label the parts. Students may want to pick up leaf specimens to tape to their illustrations. Have younger students draw a picture of a plant on their activity sheets. Help students label the parts. Display students' activity sheets on the bulletin board.

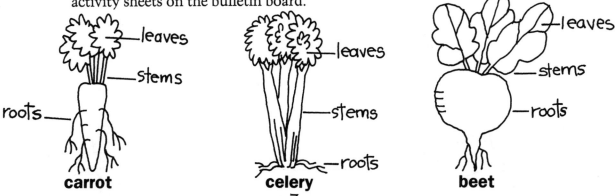

PARTS OF PLANTS

Draw a picture of different plants you saw in the park. Label the parts.

Plants Have Fruits and Seeds that Grow into Plants

Concept: Fruits contain seeds. Each seed has a tiny plant inside it. The rest of the seed is food that the tiny plant uses to grow.

Materials: For each student: raw peanut, magnifying glass, paper towel, paper cup, potting soil, lima bean or other bean seed, activity sheet (page 10).

Plan: Write the following sentence on the chalkboard or read it aloud: A seed contains a tiny plant and food for the plant to grow.

Ask students whether they think the statement is true or false and write their responses. Then tell students that they will do several experiments to learn more about seeds. After giving each student a raw peanut, a magnifying glass, and a copy of the activity sheet, tell them to open the peanut into its two halves. Then have them use the magnifying glass to observe what they find inside and record their findings on the sheet. Allow time for students to talk about their observations.

Next, give each student a paper towel and a cup, telling them to write their name on the cup. Then have each student place the dampened paper towel in the cup and a lima bean seed on the towel. Set the cups on the windowsill in indirect sunlight. Be sure to keep the paper towels moist for the duration of this experiment. Have students record their observations on their activity sheets. After several days, when the beans sprout, have students remove the paper towels, fill the cups halfway with soil, and plant the sprouted beans. Students should continue to water their plants and record their observations. Allow them time to discuss their findings.

Additional Activity: The After-Dinner Gardeners' Club! Students may enjoy bringing in seeds or pits from raw fruits and vegetables and planting them in paper cups or empty cans. Have students label the plants and observe and record their growth.

Fruits and Seeds Grow into Plants

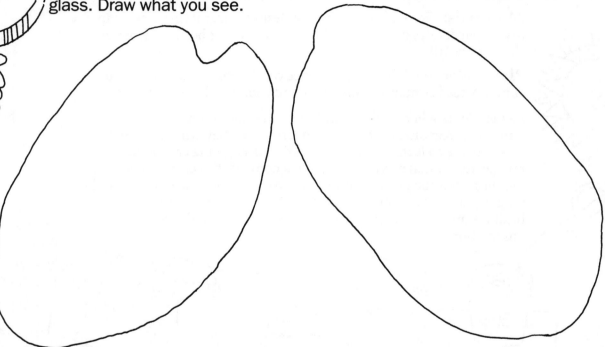

A. Open the peanut carefully. Look at the inside with your magnifying glass. Draw what you see.

B. Look at your bean seed every three days. Draw what you see.

Day __1__	Day __4__	Day __7__
Day __10__	Day __13__	

Can Plants Grow from Leaves, Stems, and Roots?

Concept: In addition to growing from seeds, some plants grow from leaves, stems, and roots.

Materials: Three glass jars, toothpicks, tape, leaf from an African violet or jade plant, stem from a philodendron, sweet potato (root), water.

Plan: Discuss with students how plants grow from seeds and fruit. Then explain that they are going to conduct an experiment to see if plants might also grow from leaves, stems, and roots. Copy the following chart onto a large piece of construction paper or have students make a copy for their science notebooks. Have students predict if plants can grow from leaves, stems, and roots. Write their predictions in the appropriate boxes.

Can plants grow from . . .

	yes	no
roots	☐	☐
stems	☐	☐
leaves	☐	☐

What we found

Roots _____

Stems _____

Leaves _____

Conclusions:_____
_____

toothpick

sweet potato

toothpick

sweet potato root

root hairs

leaf

tape

jade leaf

roots

leaf

stem

tape

roots

philodendron stem

Help students place the leaf, stem, and root in separate glasses of water. Use tape to suspend the leaf and stem over the water. Use toothpicks to suspend the sweet potato over the water. Make sure that only the parts that will root are in the water. Label each jar. Add water to the jar periodically to keep the water level constant. Place the jars in indirect sunlight.

Have students observe the plants over a two-week period. They may want to draw pictures of the plants or keep a written record of their progress. Discuss students' observations and have them draw conclusions.

What Do Plants Need to Grow?

Concept: Plants need air, sun, and water to grow.

Materials: Four small plants (can be plants students have grown in previous experiments), petroleum jelly, a recording sheet for each group.

Plan: On the chalkboard, write the words *air, water, sun.* Ask students which of these elements a plant needs to grow and write their responses. Tell students that they will do experiments to see which of these elements a plant needs.

Divide the class into four groups and give each group a plant. Group 1 will conduct an experiment to see whether a plant needs air to grow. Have the group spread petroleum jelly on the leaves and stems, explaining that this will prevent air from reaching the plant. Then tell them to place the plant in sunlight and to water it when necessary.

Group 2 will conduct an experiment to see whether a plant needs light to grow. Tell students to place the plant in a dark place, such as a closet, and to water the plant when necessary.

Group 3 will conduct an experiment to see whether a plant needs water to grow. Have them place the plant in sunlight, but *not* give it water.

Group 4 will provide its plant with sunlight, water, and air.

Have each group make a recording sheet like the one below. Groups should observe their plants daily and record their findings. After a week, have each group display its plant and report its findings to the class. Ask students to draw conclusions about what a plant needs to grow.

What we want to find:

Does a plant need _____ to grow?

What we did: _____

_____

What we saw: _____

_____

Our conclusions: _____

_____

_____

Food Comes from Plants

Concept: Much of the food we eat comes from plants.

Materials: For each student: paper cup, potting soil, crayons, alfalfa seeds, salad ingredients, paper plate.

Plan: Take students on a tour of a local greengrocer. Have them observe all the foods that come from plants and ask them to identify which part of the plant (stem, root, leaves, fruit) the various vegetables and fruit come from. After the tour, have students talk about the different foods they eat that come from plants.

Tell students that they will have an opportunity to grow their own food. Distribute paper cups, potting soil, alfalfa seeds, and crayons. Instruct students to draw funny faces on the cups and fill them almost to the top with potting soil. Have them sprinkle the alfalfa seeds on top of the soil, gently press the seeds down, and water them. Place the cups in direct sunlight. In a few days the seeds will sprout. When the seeds grow above the tops of the cups, have "Haircut and Salad Day." Distribute paper plates and salad ingredients to students, telling them to cut the alfalfa and to add it to the other ingredients to make a salad. Students will enjoy giving their reactions to eating food they have grown themselves.

Additional Activity: Plan a Meal!

Materials: Magazines, scissors, glue, construction paper.

Plan: Provide students with scissors and magazines. Have them cut out pictures of foods that come from plants. Encourage them to make collages by gluing the items to construction paper. Display students' work on the bulletin board.

Do Plants Put Water Back into the Air?

Concept: Water travels up the stem of a plant to its leaves and evaporates into the air.

Materials: For each group: two glass jars, cardboard, small amount of clay, tape, thick plant leaf with all its stems.

Plan: Remind students that a plant takes in water through its roots. Ask them to tell what they think happens to the water and write their responses on the chalkboard. Tell students that they will conduct an experiment to discover what happens to the water a plant absorbs. Divide the class into groups and distribute to each group glass jars, cardboard, clay, tape, and a plant leaf. Instruct the groups to cut the cardboard so that it is slightly bigger than the mouth of the jar. Then have them cut a small hole in the center of the cardboard, place the leaf stem through the hole, and seal the hole with clay. Next, the groups should place the cardboard on a jar filled with water. *The stem must reach into the water* (the cardboard may be taped to the side of the jar if necessary to achieve this). Have the groups place the mouth of the second jar over the leaf and then place the jars in direct sunlight. After an hour or so, the groups should observe that water droplets have formed on the inside of the top jar. Encourage the groups to discuss their observations.

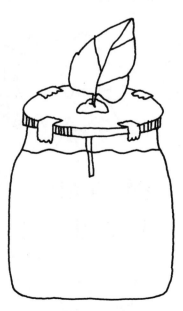

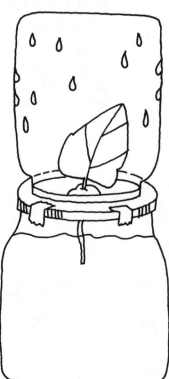

Plants Grow in Different Places

Concept: Different plants grow in the desert and in the rain forest.

Materials: Photographs of a desert and a rain forest, small cacti, tropical plants, potting soil, sandy soil (for cacti), shallow flowerpot, small glass globe or square plastic box, gravel or small stones, plastic wrap.

Plan: Display the photographs and ask students to describe the plants they see. Tell them that these are pictures of different biomes, or ecological communities. Allow students time to describe the biomes they know. Then explain that climate helps to create biomes. As one example, discuss the desert as a place that is usually hot and dry and receives very little rain. Explain that desert plants, such as cacti, have extensive networks of shallow roots that take up moisture quickly. To last them between rains, cacti store water in their tissues. Allow students time to examine the cactus plants.

As a second example of a biome, tell students that a rain forest is a hot, humid area that receives much rain. Explain that in a rain forest, plants, whose leaves are large and soft, grow in great variety. The tops of the trees interlock to form a "canopy." In a rain forest, food and water are plentiful, but plants must compete for sunlight. Allow students time to examine the tropical plants.

Students are now ready to create two biomes, a rain forest and a desert. Divide the class into two groups. Provide one group with the shallow flowerpot, gravel or small stones, cacti, and sandy potting soil. Provide the second group with the glass or plastic container, gravel or small stones, potting soil, plastic wrap, and tropical plants. (Note: the plastic wrap helps to keep the moisture level high.) Help students plant the cacti and plants according to the diagrams below. Display both terraria in the classroom and have students note periodically the progress of the plants.

plastic wrap

plants

soil

gravel

cacti

sandy soil

gravel

Making a Plant Press

Concept: A plant specimen can be preserved by pressing.

Materials: For each group: two pieces of $\frac{1}{4}$-inch (6 mm) plywood that measures 6 inches × 8 inches (15 cm × 20 cm) with a hole drilled in each corner, heavy cardboard, waxed paper, four long bolts with wing nuts, large envelopes or folders.

Plan: Ask students if they are familiar with the plants that grow naturally in their area, having them name some of the trees, bushes, and smaller plants they see around them. Tell students that a good way to find out about these plants is to go on a nature walk, collect specimens, and then preserve them by pressing them.

Have students work in groups. Provide each group with plywood, cardboard, and bolts with wing nuts. Help the groups assemble their presses according to the diagram. Insert layers of cardboard between the plywood. If you are working with younger children, you can substitute a heavy book for the press.

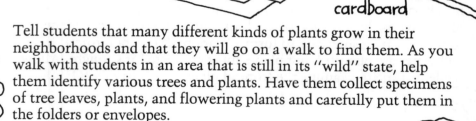

Tell students that many different kinds of plants grow in their neighborhoods and that they will go on a walk to find them. As you walk with students in an area that is still in its "wild" state, help them identify various trees and plants. Have them collect specimens of tree leaves, plants, and flowering plants and carefully put them in the folders or envelopes.

After the walk, help students press their plants. Have them carefully place their specimens between two sheets of waxed paper, making sure any leaves and petals are flat and not doubled over. Then have them place the specimens in the middle of a large book or between the layers of cardboard on their presses. When the press is full, tighten all the wing nuts evenly. Specimens should be dried within two weeks.

A Scrapbook for Flowers and Leaves

Concept: Identifying, describing, and classifying specimens are important tools in science.

Materials: Three-ring binder, poster board (cut to fit binder), clear contact paper or glue, books on trees and plants.

Plan: Tell students that they are going to make a book showing the plants that grow naturally in their area. Have groups of students use the books on trees and plants to identify the plant specimens they pressed in the previous activity. After each group writes a few sentences describing each specimen, have them glue the specimens onto the poster board (clear contact paper may be used to secure and protect dried specimens) along with the descriptions. Leaves of trees, stems and leaves of shrubs, plants, and flowering plants should be classified accordingly so that they can be displayed in corresponding sections of the book.

Help students assemble the book, complete with cover and title. Display the book in the classroom or school library.

Additional Activity: Greetings!
Students may enjoy making greeting cards using the plant specimens they pressed. Have them fold a piece of construction paper in half to make a card. Then have them glue a pressed specimen on the outside and write a greeting on the inside. Suggest to students that they send their cards to a friend or relative.

Making Recycled Paper

Concept: Plants produce oxygen that we use to breathe. Many trees are cut down to make paper. Paper can be recycled so that fewer trees need to be cut down.

Materials: For each group: bucket; wooden spoon; old newspapers; wire mesh, $1\frac{1}{2}$ feet $\times$ $1\frac{1}{2}$ feet ($\frac{1}{2}$ m $\times$ $\frac{1}{2}$ m); water.

NOTE: The day before you do this activity, soak old newspapers in water.

Plan: Discuss with students the recycling efforts people are making in your town. Explain that people today are concerned with the environment and with wasting natural resources, such as trees. Tell students that trees are important because they produce the oxygen that humans and animals need to breathe and live. Explain that since trees are used to make paper, one way of saving trees is to recycle paper. Tell students that today they will have an opportunity to make their own recycled paper.

Have students work in groups. Tell them to drain the water from the buckets and, using a wooden spoon or their hands, to mash up the newspaper. Next, students should add water to the mixture and stir it to make a mushy pulp. Using their hands, students should spread an even layer of the pulp on the wire mesh and let it dry. When the pulp is dry, have students remove it carefully from the wire mesh. They have now made recycled paper!

Additional Activity: Plant a Tree!
Arbor Day is a national holiday that makes people aware of the importance of trees to the environment. Students may enjoy beginning a campaign to plant a tree in their community. First, have them find a good location for the tree. Then help them determine who are the appropriate people to contact regarding the planting of the tree. Help students draft letters to these people. Students may wish to write their letters on the recycled paper they made earlier.

Animals Have Different Coverings

Concept: Animals have different coverings.

Materials: Different animal coverings such as skin, fur, feathers, scales, or pictures of animals with these coverings; an activity sheet for each student (page 20).

Plan: Tell students that animals have different coverings. Ask students to name the different coverings they know. If they need help, you may suggest skin, fur, feathers, or scales. Then display the animal coverings or the pictures and have students identify the various coverings as well as the animals that might have those coverings. Write students' responses on the chalkboard. You may wish to arrange the responses in diagrams like the ones that follow.

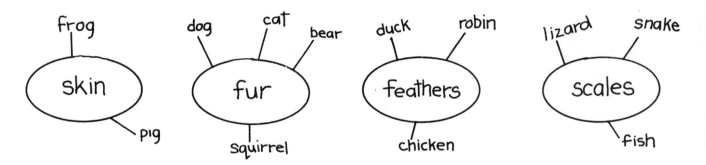

frog — skin — pig

dog / cat / bear — fur — squirrel

duck / robin — feathers — chicken

lizard / snake — scales — fish

Discuss with students why particular coverings might be useful for different animals. Then, take students on a walk to look for animals and to see what kind of coverings these animals have. Before setting out, distribute the activity sheets.

As you walk with students, help them identify various animals and their coverings. On their activity sheets, have students write the names or draw pictures of the animals they see. After the walk, discuss students' observations. Display the sheets on the bulletin board.

Name _____ Date _____

What Animals Have Skin, Fur, Feathers, Scales?

Skin

Fur

Feathers

Scales

Classifying Animals

Concept: Animal groups have basic characteristics.

Materials: Nature magazines, scissors, glue, an activity sheet for each student (page 22).

NOTE: Prepare Activity Sheet (page 22)
For Grades K–1: Before duplicating, write "Furry" under the picture of the rabbit, "Scaly" under the picture of the fish, "Feathery" under the picture of the bird, and "Scaly" under the picture of the snake.

For Grades 2–3: Before duplicating, write "Mammals" under the picture of the rabbit, "Fish" under the picture of the fish, "Birds" under the picture of the bird, and "Reptile" under the picture of the snake.

Plan: Call on volunteers to name ten to twelve animals and write the animal names on the chalkboard. Then ask students which of the animals they would group together and why. When they run out of suggestions, tell them that animal groups have basic characteristics that help people classify them.

For Grades K–1: Distribute the activity sheets, magazines, scissors, and glue. Have students identify the animals on the activity sheet and discuss the words used to describe them. Then have students find one picture of each kind of animal, cut it out, and paste it in the appropriate place on the activity sheet. Next, talk with students about how each kind of animal moves. Does it fly? Run? Swim? Crawl? Next to each picture have students write words describing the way the animal moves. Display students' activity sheets on the bulletin board.

For Grades 2–3: Have students work in groups to brainstorm some of the characteristics of the four groups of animals shown on their activity sheets. Have them consider the following: animal covering, whether the animal is warm-blooded or cold-blooded, how the animal moves, how the animal gives birth (lays eggs, has live babies).

Fish have scales cold-blooded swim most lay eggs	Mammals have fur, skin warm-blooded walk, run have live babies	Birds have feathers warm-blooded fly lay eggs	Reptiles have scales cold-blooded slither, crawl most lay eggs

After deciding on the characteristics of each group, have students record them on their activity sheets. They may also want to list other animals that might be found in each group. Allow each group time to present its findings.

Name _____ Date _____

Classifying Animals Activity Sheet

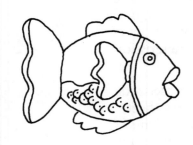

Animals Need Food, Air, and Water

Concept: Animals need food, air, and water to live.

Materials: Two earthworms (from soil in your neighborhood or from a local bait-and-tackle shop), large wide-mouthed jar with a lid, soil, sand, lettuce, cabbage, carrot scrapings, spray bottle with water, an activity sheet for each student (page 24).

Plan: Discuss with students what things they need to live. After they have responded, write *food*, *air*, and *water* on the chalkboard. Ask students which of these elements *all* animals need to live. Then tell them that they will conduct an experiment to find out if all animals need air, water and food to live. Tell students that they will use earthworms in their experiment. (Explain that although they are small, earthworms play an important role in the environment. Earthworms burrow and gnaw their way through the soil, aerating the soil and bringing new soil to the surface.)

Help students set up the experiment, reminding them that worms are delicate creatures and need to be handled carefully.

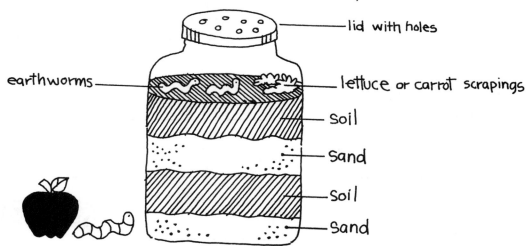

First, fill the jar with alternating layers of sand and soil. Next, punch five or six air holes in the lid. Place vegetable scrapings in the jar and sprinkle with water. Then put in the earthworms. Keep the jar away from light.

Distribute activity sheets and have students make predictions. They may also draw pictures of the contents of the jar. Have them observe the worms for a week. (Don't forget to leave food for the worms and spray them with water daily.) After a week, ask students to draw what the contents of the jar look like now. Help students record their observations and draw conclusions.

When the experiment is completed, return earthworms to the outdoors.

Do Animals Need Food, Air, and Water?

What does the inside look like?

	yes	no
Water		
Food		
Air		

What I found _____

_____

_____

What I think _____

_____

_____

_____

_____

What does the inside look like now?

_____

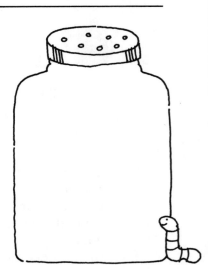

Animals Live in Different Places

Concept: Animals make homes in many different places.

Materials: Magazine pictures showing animals living in various places, for example, a bear in a den, a fish in water, a bird in a tree, a rabbit in a burrow; large poster board, crayons.

Additional Activity: bird's nest or picture of bird's nest, twigs, bits of paper, string or wool, dried grass, construction paper, and scissors (optional).

NOTE: Use the poster board to make a chart like the following.

Animal	Where we saw it
🐰	🐰 (in grass)

Plan: Discuss with students the idea that animals live in different places. Display the magazine pictures and ask students to describe the animals shown and their homes. Ask for examples of other animals and where they live. Tell students that they will go on a walk to look for animals and to find out where they live. Before the walk, have students predict what animals they might see and where they might see them.

On the walk, help students identify various animals. Don't forget small animals, such as ants, worms, and honeybees. Afterward, have students record their observations on the chart. Allow time for students to discuss their findings. During the next few weeks, as they find other animals, encourage students to add them to the chart.

Additional Activity: Making a Bird's Nest
Display a bird's nest. Explain that birds make nests by weaving together twigs and other materials, adding bits of mud for strength, and lining the structure with softer material.

Have students work in pairs. Tell each pair to gather twigs, bits of string or wool, dried grass, and strips of paper. Then have them work together to weave their materials into a bird's nest. Some students may enjoy cutting paper birds and eggs from construction paper to place in their nests. Display the nests in the classroom.

My Naturalist's Diary

Concept: A naturalist observes animals and their behavior.

Materials: For each student: construction paper to make a naturalist's diary.

Plan: Ask students to describe some of the things they have noticed about their house pets, squirrels in the park, or other animals. Explain to students that when they observe animals they are doing a naturalist's job. Tell them that a naturalist studies animals and their behavior and then writes or draws his or her observations.

Tell students that they, too, can be naturalists. Distribute construction paper on which students can draw pictures and write their findings for several animals they choose to observe. Tell students that as they observe their animals they should try to answer the following questions:

1. What is the animal?
2. What does it look like? (color, shape, and so on)
3. Where does it live?
4. Does it live with a family or alone?
5. What is the animal doing?

Allow students several weeks in which to make their observations and to record them. Help students to construct their diaries by stapling together their sheets of construction paper. Tell students to prepare covers for their books, entitled *My Naturalist's Diary*. Give each student time to present his or her findings to the class. You may wish to display the diaries in the classroom or make a special exhibit in the school library.

Hatching Frog Eggs

Concept: Frogs lay eggs that hatch into tadpoles. Tadpoles develop into frogs.

Materials: Frog eggs, pond water, pond algae, pond plants, bucket, mealworms (if you intend to keep frog), large rock, screen mesh, aquarium, an activity sheet for each student (page 28).

Plan: Explain to students that in the spring, amphibians such as frogs, toads, and salamanders go to swamps and ponds to lay their eggs. Tell students that they will observe the various stages of development as frog eggs develop into tadpoles and then into adult frogs.

If there is a pond or swamp area nearby, go there with students (bring the bucket) and try to find frog eggs to bring back to the classroom. (You may also find toad or salamander eggs.) If this is not possible, you may order frog eggs from a science supply house (see page v for information). Bring back eggs of only one species, for mixing eggs could result in one species eating the other.

Distribute the activity sheet and have students observe and record in words or pictures how the eggs grow and change. The eggs should change into small tadpoles within a week to ten days. Keep several tadpoles to observe, returning the others and any unhatched eggs to the pond.

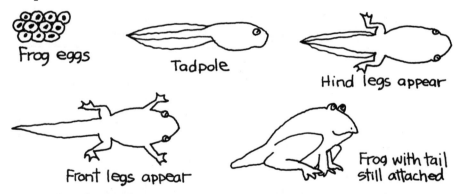

Frog eggs

Tadpole

Hind legs appear

Front legs appear

Frog with tail still attached

For each tadpole, discuss with students the various stages of frog development, noting when the hind legs appear, when the front legs appear, and when the tails disappear. Once the tails disappear, move the frogs to an aquarium in which there is a large rock. Place a screen mesh over the aquarium to make sure the frogs don't jump out. At this point, feed the frogs the mealworms.

After students have made their final observations, return the frogs to the pond. Students may add their observation sheets to their naturalist's diaries or keep them in their science notebooks.

Name _____   Date _____

Hatching Frog Eggs

Observe the frog's development from egg to adult. Record your findings in words or pictures.

Day 1	Day 3	Day 5
Day 8	Day 10	Day 12
Day 14	Day 18	Day 24
Day ___	Day ___	Day ___

Making Bird Feeders

Concept: Bird feeders will attract the birds native to an area. Simple bird feeders can be made from recycled objects.

Materials: For each student: pine cone, spoon, peanut butter, newspaper, wild birdseed, string OR for each group: empty coffee can, can opener, two aluminum pie plates, wire, wild birdseed, an activity sheet for each student (page 30).

Plan: Tell students that bird feeders attract birds. Explain that by making simple bird feeders and hanging them outdoors, they will be able to observe and record what birds live in their area.

Provide students or groups with the materials. To make the pine cone feeders, have students tie a 12″ length of string securely around the top of the pine cone. They may then use the spoon to mush peanut butter between the pine cone scales. Spread a newspaper over a desk and pour birdseed onto it. Have students roll the pine cones in the birdseed. Students may then hang their feeders on tree branches within viewing distance of classroom windows.

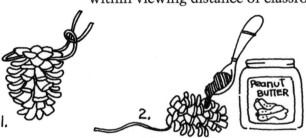

To make recycled feeders, punch two holes in each of the pie plates and the bottom of the coffee can as shown. Using a can opener, make three holes in the sides of the coffee can at the bottom. Using wire, assemble bird feeder as shown. Fill coffee can halfway with birdseed. Hang feeders from trees or outside classroom windows.

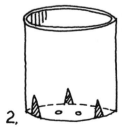

Distribute activity sheets to students. Have them observe the various birds (or other animals) that feed at the feeder and the dates and times they feed. Obtain bird books from the school library so that students can identify the birds and learn about their habits.

Have students discuss their observations.

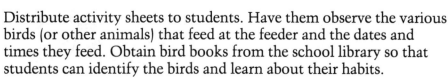

Name _____ Date _____

What I Saw at the Bird Feeder

Keep a record of the birds or other animals you see feeding at the bird feeder. You may draw pictures if you wish.

Date	Time	What I Saw

Growing and Changing

Concept: As humans grow, they become taller and heavier. Children resemble their parents.

Materials: Students' baby pictures or pictures of babies from magazines; construction-paper cutouts and crayons for each student. *Additional Activity:* wire hanger, construction-paper cutouts, crayons, string, and tape for each student.

Plan: Display the baby pictures to the class and have them describe how they looked when they were babies and how they have changed since then. Talk about how they have grown taller and heavier and how they have developed many skills, such as walking, talking, running, writing, and reading. Explain that some characteristics, such as eye color and skin color, will not change as they get older, for these characteristics are inherited from their parents. Discuss with students in what ways they look like their parents.

Prepare cutouts from construction paper and distribute them and crayons to students. After asking students to imagine what they will look like when they are adults, have them draw that image on their cutout. Label the cutouts with each student's name and display them on the bulletin board.

Additional Activity: Family Mobiles
Help students make mobiles that show their family units. Ask students to name the members of their family and their relationship. Tell them they are going to make mobiles showing their family units. Prepare a mobile in advance so that students will have an idea of what the finished product will look like. Distribute cutouts, crayons, string, tape, and a wire hanger to each student. Have students use a cutout to depict each family member, using crayons to add such details as hair, facial features, and clothing. Next tell students to tape a piece of string to the back of each cutout, tie the other end of the string to the hanger, and reinforce the connection with tape. Display the family mobiles in one area of the classroom.

The Nose Knows

Concept: Things have different odors. We use our noses to smell and identify objects.

Materials: Four paper cups and four cotton balls (one soaked in perfume, one soaked in sour milk, one containing several drops of peppermint extract, and one in which a garlic clove has been crushed).

Plan: Ask students to imagine that it is a beautiful spring day. The flowers are all in bloom, and the sun is shining brightly. Ask them what is the first thing they do when they walk outside. If students don't mention it, suggest that one thing might be to take a deep breath of air. Next, ask them what they smell when they take a deep breath (flowers, the freshness of the air). Explain that the sense of smell in humans and most animals makes them able to identify odors and to tell them apart. After asking students to tell what body part helps them to smell, have them name some odors. Tell students that they are about to do an experiment in which they use their noses and their sense of smell to identify certain odors.

Label the cups 1, 2, 3, 4, and put one cotton ball in each cup. Divide class into four groups. Distribute a cup to each group. After groups have had a chance to identify the smell, have them switch cups. Continue until each group has had an opportunity to identify the smell in each cup. Have groups record their findings in a chart like the one below and then have them present their findings. Ask students to name other foods or items that have the same odor as those in the cups.

Cup	What we smelled
1	
2	
3	
4	

Hearing and Our Ears

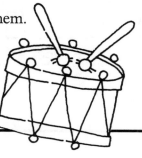

Concept: We use our ears to identify sounds and their locations.

Materials: Homemade audiotape of different sounds, including alarm clock ringing, telephone ringing, school bell ringing, dog barking, kitchen appliance turning on, whistle, siren, and other distinctive yet familiar sounds; for each group: empty coffee cans with lids; different types of objects, such as marble, penny, pencil, eraser.

Plan: Tell students that you are going to play a tape recording and that they are to listen carefully and tell what sounds they hear. Play one sound at a time, stopping after each to give students a chance to identify the sound. After you have played the whole tape, discuss the sense of hearing with students. Explain that humans and most animals hear with their ears and that the sense of hearing makes them able to identify sounds, their locations, and their directions. Tell students that knowing the direction and location of a sound is very important. To illustrate this, press your thumb and index finger together, telling students that this represents a bumblebee. Next make a buzzing sound as you walk away from students. Ask them to point to the location and direction of the sound. Now walk toward students, continuing to make the buzzing sound. Ask them to point to the location and direction. Explain that the location and direction of sound make us aware of things around us. If we heard a bee buzzing a few yards away, we wouldn't be worried, but if that same bee was buzzing in our ear, we might want to get away from it.

Tell students that they are going to experiment with location and direction of sound. Divide the class into groups and provide each group with an empty coffee can and a different object. (This is done so that each can will make a unique sound and students will not be confused by the sounds made by other groups.) For each group, instruct one student to sit in a chair with his or her eyes closed while another student shakes the can containing the object. The seated student must describe the location and direction of the sound. The student shaking the can may move behind, in front of, or to either side of the seated student, either far away or up close. (Caution students not to shake the can too close to the ears of the seated student.) Make sure each student has an opportunity to be a "shaker" and a "sitter." Afterward, discuss students' observations with them. Have them suggest how knowing the location and direction of a sound can help them be aware of things around them.

How Do the Hearing Impaired Communicate?

Concept: People who are hearing impaired often use sign language to communicate.

Plan: Tell students that there are many people who hear poorly or not at all. Explain that although some of these people wear hearing aids, devices that make sound louder, others rely on sign language to communicate. Ask students to tell about any experiences they have had with sign language. Tell students that they are going to learn how to communicate with sign language. Use the following illustration to help students to use their fingers and arms to communicate.

Happy   Birth   Day   I am

five   Six   Seven   Eight

What Different Tastes Can the Tongue Identify?

Concept: The tongue can taste salty, bitter, sweet, spicy, or sour food.

Materials: Sour pickle, chili powder, salty potato chip, small piece of bitter chocolate, gumdrop, chart made from poster board, magazines, scissors, glue.
Additional Activity: for each student: mirror, salt, brown sugar.

NOTE: Prepare a chart like the following before beginning this activity.

Salty	Sweet	Sour	Bitter	Spicy

Plan: Ask students to name some of their favorite lunch foods and to describe what they taste like. Explain that our tongues have the sense of taste, which helps us to identify the taste of food. Help students name the five tastes: salty, bitter, sweet, sour, and spicy. Display the five foods and help students identify which is salty, bitter, sweet, sour, and spicy. Next show students the chart, telling them that they are going to look through magazines to find and cut out pictures of foods that fit into each of these categories. Provide small groups of students with magazines and scissors. Groups should find one food for each category. When groups have finished, allow them time to discuss their pictures and to glue them in the appropriate space on the chart. Display the chart on the bulletin board.

Additional Activity: What part of the tongue can taste sugar? Salt?

Provide students with mirrors. Have them look in the mirrors and stick out their tongues. Explain that the tiny bumps they see on their tongues are taste buds and that taste buds help to identify the taste of foods. Tell students that each section of the tongue can taste a different flavor. Help students determine which part of the tongue can taste sugar and which part can taste salt. After giving students some salt and brown sugar, have them place a tiny bit of salt in their mouth and "rinse" it around their tongue. Draw an outline of a tongue on the chalkboard. Point to the tip, the sides, and the back of the tongue and ask students in which of these areas they tasted the salt. Repeat the procedure with sugar. Allow students time to discuss their findings.

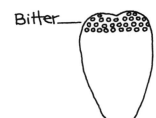

Bitter

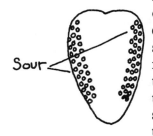

Sour

Salty

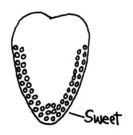

Sweet

Our Sense of Touch

Concept: Our sense of touch allows us to determine different textures: roughness, smoothness, softness, and hardness.

Materials: Four large, clear plastic bags, chart made from poster board, four objects such as block of wood (hard), emery board (rough), a glass paperweight (smooth), piece of fabric (soft).

Plan: Pass the objects around to students and have them describe how the objects feel. Help them to identify smooth, rough, soft, and hard. Explain to them that our skin has the sense of touch. Our skin helps us know when an object is soft, hard, smooth, or rough. It can sense when an object is dull or sharp. Ask students to think of other sensations our skin can feel (hot, cold, wet, dry). Divide the poster board into four sections as shown. Label each section and staple a plastic bag in each.

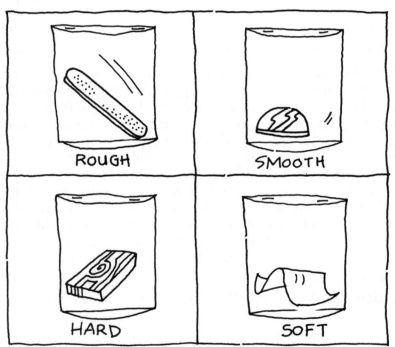

Take students for a walk in the neighborhood to find and collect items that fit into each of the four categories. Upon returning to the classroom, allow students time to share their items with classmates. Give them the opportunity to discuss the characteristics of the items and to touch them. Then help students decide in which bag each item belongs. Display the chart on the bulletin board.

Over the next few weeks, encourage students to bring in items from home that fit into the categories on the chart. Have students present these to the class and decide in which bag each belongs.

How Do We Use Our Eyes?

Concept: Our eyes provide us with the sense of sight.

Materials: Large picture containing many small pictures cut from a magazine, a small amount of clay formed into two balls.

Plan: Hold up a pencil and ask students to describe it. Tell them that our eyes provide us with the sense of sight, which makes us able to see an object and determine its color, shape, and size, as well as how far away it is from us. Tell students they will do experiments to learn more about their sense of sight.

1. Explain to students that although we think we have a wide picture of the world in front of us, in reality we can focus on only one small spot at a time. To demonstrate this, give one student the picture, asking him or her to focus on only one item or object in it. Then ask the student to try to identify some of the other items or objects in the picture *without moving his or her eyes.* Call on other students to try to do the same. Finally, involve the whole class in the experiment by telling them to focus on something on the opposite side of the classroom. Then ask them to try to see objects around their focus point *without moving their eyes.* Allow students time to share reactions and to form conclusions.

2. Explain to students that although people cannot see behind them without turning around, they can see to their sides. Tell them that this side vision is called "peripheral vision." With a volunteer, demonstrate to the class how they can test their peripheral vision. Clear a space in the classroom. Have the volunteer take a small clay ball in each hand and look straight ahead. Beginning with arms behind them and at shoulder level, have the volunteer slowly bring arms forward. Tell the volunteer to stop moving his or her arms when the fingers come into view and to drop the clay to mark that spot. Allow all students an opportunity to test their peripheral vision. Afterward, discuss their observations with them. Ask students how peripheral vision might help them as they walk to or from school.

Making a Stethoscope

Concept: A stethoscope can amplify the sound a heart makes.

Materials: For each group: funnel, two feet of rubber tubing (available in hardware stores), tape OR cardboard tubing from a roll of paper towels, watch with second hand.

Plan: Talk with students about how the heart pumps blood throughout the body and why it is an important organ. Ask them to recall how a doctor listens to their hearts. If necessary, display a picture of a stethoscope. Tell students that doctors use a stethoscope to find out if a person's heart is beating properly. A stethoscope makes the sound of the heart louder. During a heartbeat the heart will make two noises; one is the sound of the heart valves opening and the other is the sound of the heart valves closing. Tell students that when they listen to a heart they will hear pit-PAT, pit-PAT, pit-PAT.

Have students work in small groups. Have each group make a stethoscope by inserting the funnel into the end of the rubber tubing and taping the two together, if necessary.

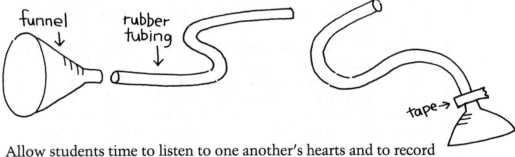

Allow students time to listen to one another's hearts and to record the number of times a heart beats in a minute (younger students might just listen for the heartbeat).

After the activity, discuss students' findings.

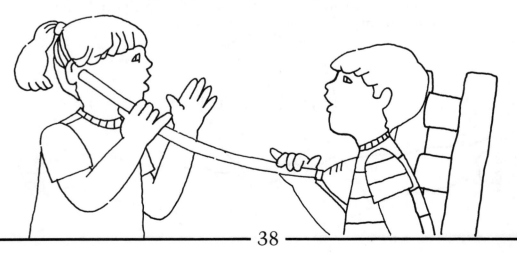

Name _____ Date _____

Heart Stress Test

Our heart rate, or the number of times a minute our heart beats, varies depending on how active we are. Work with a partner. Take turns doing the activities listed on the chart. Use your stethoscope and a watch with a second hand to check your heart beat after each activity. Be sure to catch your breath between activities. Record your findings.

Heart Rate (number of heart beats per minute)

	50	60	70	80	90	100	110	120	130	140	150	160	170	180
Sitting														
Swinging arms (20 seconds)														
Walking (30 seconds)														
Hopping (25 hops)														
Running in place (30 seconds)														
Standing														

My heart beat fastest when I _____

My heart beat slowest when I _____

Are Some Foods More Harmful to Teeth than Others?

Concept: Some foods are more harmful to teeth than other foods are. Brushing the teeth regularly can remove bacteria and food particles that cause tooth decay.

Materials: For each group: activity sheet (page 41); glass; tooth (ask students to bring in baby teeth they have lost or order artificial teeth from a science supply company); and soda, water, fruit juice, or carrot juice.

Plan: Ask students to tell if they think certain foods are more harmful to their teeth than others and, if so, to name them. Tell them they will do an experiment to learn how harmful certain liquids are to their teeth. Divide the class into groups and provide each group with an activity sheet. Next, give each group a tooth; a glass; and some soda, juice, or water. Ask students to predict which of the liquids they think is most harmful. Tell students to draw a picture of the tooth in the box marked Day 1 on the activity sheet and then to drop the tooth into the glass and fill the glass with the liquid. Every two days, have students use a spoon to remove the tooth from the glass, check the tooth, and record their observations by drawing in the appropriate box. After the experiment, have each group present its observations to the rest of the class. Then have the class discuss their findings and draw conclusions about the connection between food and tooth decay.

This experiment can be a good way to remind students that brushing and flossing teeth remove food particles, bacteria, and plaque, which can cause teeth to decay.

Are Some Foods More Harmful to Teeth than Others?

Are some foods more harmful to teeth than other foods?

What we predict: yes ☐   no ☐

Our glass contains _____.

What we observed:

Day 1	**Day 3**	**Day 5**	**Day 7**
Day 9	**Day 11**	**Day 13**	**Day 15**

What we found: _____
_____

Our conclusion: _____
_____

Testing for Fat, Starch, and Protein

Concept: Our bodies need three basic categories of food. We can test foods to see if they contain protein, carbohydrates, and fats.

Materials: Small amount of butter, salad oil, peanut butter, bread, gumdrops, raw potato, cheese, hardboiled egg, chart made from poster board.

For the fat test: In addition to the above foods, a large brown bag cut into small squares, flashlight.
For the carbohydrate test: In addition to the above foods, tincture of iodine.
For the protein test: In addition to the above foods, potassium or sodium hydroxide, copper sulfate solution, eight small glass jars.

NOTE: Prepare a chart like the following before conducting this activity.

Plan: Discuss with students some of the foods they eat for lunch. Explain to them that there are three basic categories of food that they need for their bodies to run properly. The first category is protein, which helps the body to grow and repair itself. Foods containing protein include meat, cheese, eggs, and beans. The second category is carbohydrates, which provide quick energy for the body. Carbohydrates include bread, rice, pasta, candy, potatoes, and cereal. Fats, the third category, also produce energy for the body, energy that is often stored for long periods of time. Fats include butter, salad oil, mayonnaise, and margarine. Help students name other foods that fit into these three categories. Tell them that they will do experiments to test whether a food item contains fat, carbohydrates, or protein.

Assemble the foods. Test for fat first. Call on volunteers to rub each food carefully on a square of brown paper. Let the paper dry and then shine the flashlight on the back of the paper. Allow students to examine the paper. If fat is present, the light will shine through. Tell students to put a check mark on the chart if the food contains fat. To test for carbohydrates, put a drop of tincture of iodine on each of the foods. If the food contains carbohydrates, the iodine will turn bluish black. Have students make their observations and put a check mark on the chart if the food is a carbohydrate. To test for protein, put a solution of potassium (or sodium hydroxide) into each of the glass jars and add one food item to each jar. Dilute the copper sulfate solution and add a few drops to each jar. If the food contains protein, the solution will turn pink or blue. Have students make their observations and mark their findings on the chart. Allow students time to discuss their findings. Help them note that some foods belong to more than one category.

Food	Fat	Carbohydrates	Protein
Butter			
Bread			
Eggs			
Cheese			
Peanut butter			
Gumdrops			
Potato			
Salad oil			

What Covers the Earth?

Concept: The earth is covered by land and water.

Materials: Variety of pictures cut from magazines showing mountain, hill, valley, river, stream, pond, grassy plain, and ocean; globe; activity sheet (page 44) for each student.

Plan: Display the pictures for students and have them describe what they see. After having them identify which of the pictures show water and which show land, bring out the globe and help them identify the water and the land masses on it. Tell students that they are going to learn what covers the earth. Distribute an activity sheet to each student. Read the question aloud and tell students to record their answers.

If possible, take students to the top of a hill, where they can look out over the land. If this is not possible, take them on a walk where they can see various land formations and different bodies of water. Have them record their observations by drawing or writing about what they see. Afterward, have them talk about the the kinds of land and water they saw. Ask them whether their answers on the activity sheets were correct. Display the activity sheets on the bulletin board along with pictures of various types of land and water masses.

Name _____ Date _____

What Covers the Earth?

Do land and water cover the earth?

yes ☐ no ☐

What I found (draw or write what you see):

My conclusion: _____

_____

_____

What Is Soil Made Of?
——What Does Soil Contain?——

Concept: Soil contains many things, including rock, sand, decomposing leaves, twigs, and insects.

Materials: *For each student:* tweezer, small paper cup containing soil, magnifying glass, newspapers, activity sheet (page 46).

WHAT DOES SOIL CONTAIN?	
MY PREDICTIONS	WHAT I FOUND

Plan: Discuss soil with students, having them identify some of its characteristics. Tell students that today they are going to examine soil to determine what soil contains. Have them predict what they will find and write their predictions in chart form on the chalkboard.

Have students work individually. Spread newspapers on desks and distribute materials. Have students pour the contents of the cups on the newspapers. Then tell them to use the tweezers and their hands to find rocks, twigs, decomposing leaves, dirt, and insects, such as worms, grubs, and ants. Have them put what they find in the appropriate circles on their activity sheets. Encourage students to use the magnifying glasses to examine the soil more closely and to look for very small insects.

After students have finished, allow them time to discuss their findings and share their reactions. Have them compare their findings with their predictions.

What Does Soil Contain?

rocks

twigs
&
leaves

small animals
&
insects

sand

other

How Do Rocks Wear Down to Make Soil?

Concept: Rocks wear down into soil through erosion caused by wind and water.

Materials: For each group: rocks (soft rocks work best), plastic jar with lid, water, cheesecloth, white paper.

Plan: Ask students to recall the experiment on soil composition and to name some of the things that soil is made of. Then display two rocks, reminding students that they saw rocks in the soil they examined. Explain to students that wind, rain, snow, ice, and water all help to break down rocks into soil. Tell them they will conduct two experiments to see how rocks wear down into soil.

Have students work in groups and provide each group with rocks, paper, a plastic jar, water, and cheesecloth. Next, tell students that in nature, rocks move; they tumble down hills and hit other rocks and trees. Explain that when this happens, friction helps to wear down the rocks. Have all members of each group take two rocks and rub them together over the white paper. Ask groups to note their findings on the paper.

Next, explain to students that the constantly moving water in oceans and rivers also helps to wear down rocks. Have students put two rocks in a jar, fill it halfway with water, and close it tightly. Have students take turns shaking the jar vigorously for about ten minutes. Then have them open the jar, remove the rocks, and strain the contents through cheesecloth. Have them examine the residue left on the cheesecloth and record their findings. Allow students time to talk about their observations and draw conclusions based on their findings.

We Can Help Prevent Erosion

Concept: Erosion causes valuable soil to wash away. Plants can prevent soil from eroding.

Materials: Picture from a magazine showing badly eroded land; two small flowerpots, one containing packed soil, the other a houseplant (one that is rootbound is best for this experiment); two metal baking pans; mound of soil for each pan; sticks; rocks; grass and weeds (with roots) gathered from outside; two spray water bottles filled with water; newspaper; grass seed; flower seed.
Note: A few days before doing this experiment, have students put a mound of dirt in each metal pan. (The mounds should be of equal size.) Next, have them plant the grass and weeds on the sides of one of the mounds and water carefully. Sticks and rocks may be placed on the sides of both mounds. Allow a few days for the plants to take root.

Plan: Place newspaper on a desk and display the two flowerpots. As students watch, take the pot without the plant and turn it over into the palm of your hand. Then take the pot containing the plant and gently remove the plant (roots and all) from it. Ask students to identify which flower pot contained soil that held together and to tell how they think the dirt was held together. Have students examine the plant to see that the roots are holding the soil in place.

Next, display the picture showing land erosion, explaining that wind and rain can erode land. Tell students that when land erodes, layers of rich soil are washed away, making it difficult for plants to grow in the poor soil that is left. Ask students why it is important to prevent soil from eroding. Tell them that they will conduct an experiment to see how to prevent soil erosion.

Have students take turns holding the water bottles over the mounds and spraying them with water. Make sure an equal amount of water is sprayed on each mound. Have students spray until it is clear that the soil in the mound that does not have plants is washing away. When the experiment is over, have students share their observations. Lead them to conclude that the soil in the second mound washed away because there were no roots holding the soil together. The soil in the first mound had plant roots holding the soil together and, therefore, the mound did not erode.

Ask students to think about places in their neighborhood where no plants are growing. Plan a planting party with them. Provide each student with grass seed or flower seed. Visit the areas, plant your seeds, and water them. Return periodically with students to check the progress of plants and to determine how the land or soil changed because of the plants.

How Are Salt Water and Fresh Water Different?

Concept: Salt water and fresh water have different properties.

Materials: For each group: salt, water, two drinking glasses, teaspoon, labels, two small pieces of cork, magnifying glass, chart (see below). *For additional activity:* clear plastic bottle with cap, water, salad oil, blue food coloring.

	Salt Water	Fresh Water
How does it look?		
How does it taste?		
Does a cork float in it?		

Plan: Ask students to tell what they know about ocean water. Explain that ocean water is different from the fresh water that is in streams, rivers, and ponds—ocean water contains salt, and fresh water does not. Tell students that today they will do some experiments to see how salt water and fresh water are different. Have students work in groups. Provide each group with materials and a copy of the chart. Tell students to fill each glass 2/3 full with water and then to put 2 heaping teaspoons of salt in one glass and stir until it is dissolved. After they label the glasses "salt water" and "fresh water," have students use the magnifying glass to examine how the water in each glass looks. Next, have the members of each group taste the water. Then have them try floating a piece of cork in each glass. Have students record their observations on the chart and allow them time to discuss their findings.

Additional Activity: Make Waves!

This simple experiment will help students get an idea of how waves crest and break. Fill the bottle about 1/3 full with salad oil. Then fill to the top with water. Add a few drops of blue food coloring. Screw the cap tightly on the bottle and place the bottle on its side. Have students gently rock the bottle forward and backward to create an ocean wave. Make sure each student has a chance to create waves.

How Can Water Be Cleaned?

Concept: Different methods must be used to remove particles, including pollutants, from water.

Materials: For each group: a large bowl half filled with "polluted" water (which contains twigs, leaves, rocks, bits of Styrofoam, and salad oil), tweezers, strainer, plastic spoons, paper towels, large container, activity sheet (page 51).

Plan: Talk about water pollution with students. Have them tell about some things that make water dirty and about why they would or would not like to cook with, drink, or wash in polluted water. Tell students that today they will work in groups to clean polluted water.

After distributing materials and activity sheets to groups, tell them to discuss the methods they might use to clean the water and to write their ideas on their activity sheets. Then have them try each method and write their findings on the sheets. If students have difficulty getting started, you might suggest the following:

● Using tweezers and the spoons, remove the twigs, leaves, rocks, and Styrofoam.

● Strain polluted water into second container.

● Gently place paper towels on top of the water to remove salad oil.

After students have completed the activity, allow them time to discuss their findings. Have groups compare their water. Help students draw conclusions about the difficulty of cleaning water once it is polluted.

How Can Water Be Cleaned?

Draw or write how the water looked before you started.

What we did to clean the water	How the water looked afterward

What Tells Us that the Air Is Moving?

Concept: Air has a force. This force helps keep kites afloat.

Materials: Fan, piece of paper, picture of a kite, hang glider, or parachute cut from a magazine. For each group: parachute made with a square paper napkin, thread, paper clip. **NOTE:** Make parachutes by folding the tissue paper as shown. Attach opposite corners with thread. Hang a paper clip where the threads meet.

How to make a parachute

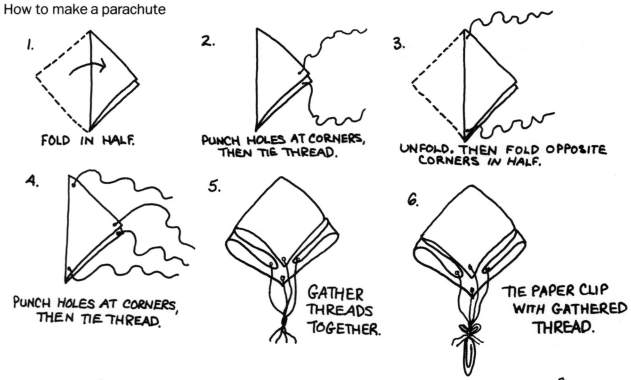

1. FOLD IN HALF.

2. PUNCH HOLES AT CORNERS, THEN TIE THREAD.

3. UNFOLD, THEN FOLD OPPOSITE CORNERS IN HALF.

4. PUNCH HOLES AT CORNERS, THEN TIE THREAD.

5. GATHER THREADS TOGETHER.

6. TIE PAPER CLIP WITH GATHERED THREAD.

Plan: Display the piece of paper to students. Then turn on the fan and place the paper in front of it. Ask students to tell what is causing the paper to move. Explain to students that although the air is invisible, the effect of it on the paper can be seen. Ask students to go to the window, look outside, and name the things they see that move because of the air. Write students' responses on the chalkboard.

Explain that air is also a force that helps to keep things afloat. Display a picture of a kite, a hang glider, or a parachute and tell students that they will conduct an experiment to see how air can keep something afloat. Have students work in groups. Provide each group with a parachute. Have students take turns gently holding the parachute above their heads and letting it go. Have them observe what happens to the parachute. After each student has had a chance to drop the parachute, discuss their observations with them and help them to draw conclusions about air.

How Clean Is the Air?

Concept: Although air is invisible, it can contain particles of dirt, dust, and other pollutants.

Materials: Picture showing smog hanging over a city or a factory spewing soot into the air. For each group: two jar lids, spoon, petroleum jelly, magnifying glass, activity sheet (page 54).

Plan: Ask students to describe what they see in the air. After they have given their responses, explain that although air seems to be invisible, it can contain many small particles, such as dirt, dust, and other pollutants. Display the picture and ask students to think about what happens to the dirt and dust particles that get into the air. Tell them that they will conduct an experiment to discover just how clean the air is.

Have students work in groups and provide each group with the jar lids, spoon, petroleum jelly, magnifying glass, and activity sheet. Have groups fill both jar lids with a layer of petroleum jelly and then place one lid somewhere in the classroom. Have them place the other lid outside on the windowsill or somewhere on the school grounds where it will not be disturbed. On their activity sheets, have students write their predictions about what will collect in the lids. Each day have groups use magnifying glasses to examine their lids and write or draw their findings.

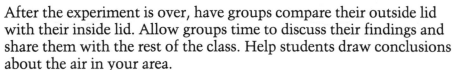

After the experiment is over, have groups compare their outside lid with their inside lid. Allow groups time to discuss their findings and share them with the rest of the class. Help students draw conclusions about the air in your area.

Name _____ Date _____

How Clean Is the Air?

We predict the air outside is   clean ☐   dirty ☐ .

We predict the air inside is   clean ☐   dirty ☐ .

What we found: **Outside**   **Inside**

Day 1 ⃝ ⃝

Day 2 ⃝ ⃝

Day 3 ⃝ ⃝

Day 4 ⃝ ⃝

Our conclusion: _____

_____

_____

54

How Do We Use Land, Air, and Water?

Concept: People use land, air, and water in many different ways.

Materials: Large sheet of mural paper, construction paper, glue, crayons, activity sheet (page 56) for each student.

Plan: On the chalkboard, write the headings "Land," "Water," and "Air." Then have students imagine that they are on a family outing to a beach. The sun is shining brightly, the water is blue and sparkling, and the sand is warm under their feet. Ask students to imagine all the things they can do at the beach. Write their suggestions on the chalkboard under the appropriate heading. If students do not mention it themselves, you may suggest flying a kite or playing Frisbee as activities that involve air. Tell students that they will be going for a walk in the neighborhood, during which they will look for ways people use land, air, and water. Distribute activity sheets to students.

Take students on a tour of the neighborhood and help them identify ways people use land, air, and water. Students should draw or write their observations on their activity sheets. On returning to the classroom, have students discuss their findings. Help them use those findings to make a mural showing how people use land, air, and water. Use construction paper to make cutouts of bodies of water, land masses, buildings, trees, and the like. Have students work in groups and give each group several cutouts and crayons. Tell them to use the crayons to add details to the cutouts. Glue the cutouts to the mural paper. Encourage students who think of other uses to include those uses on the mural. Display the mural on a bulletin board in the school corridor or in the classroom.

How Do We Use Land, Air, and Water?

Land	Air	Water

Is It Hotter in the Sun or in the Shade?

Concept: It is cooler when an object blocks the direct rays of the sun.

Materials: Two thermometers (Fahrenheit or Celsius), two cups filled with water. *For each student:* red and blue crayons, activity sheet (page 58).

Plan: Ask students to describe a time when the weather was very warm and have them tell if they felt more comfortable in the sun or in the shade. Tell students that they will conduct two experiments to determine if it is hotter in the sun or in the shade. Choose a sunny day to do these experiments. Distribute an activity sheet to each student.

Display the thermometers. Tell students that they will record the temperatures first at the beginning of the experiment and then at hourly intervals for two hours after placing one thermometer in the shade and the other in the sun. Label one thermometer "shade" and the other "sun." Have a volunteer read the temperature of one of the thermometers and demonstrate how the temperature is noted on the activity sheet.

Tell students that they will also use paper cups filled with water to determine if it is hotter in the sun or the shade. Take students outside. Place one thermometer in a cup of water in direct sunlight. Place the other thermometer in another cup of water in the shade. Return with students every hour for two hours and have them note and record the temperature shown on each thermometer. After the experiment with the thermometers is over, tell students to feel the water in each cup to determine which is hotter and to record their findings by coloring on their activity sheets with the appropriate crayon. Have students review their findings and draw conclusions about whether it is hotter in the sun or in the shade.

Name _____ Date _____

Is It Hotter in the Sun or in the Shade?

What I Predict:

It is hotter in the   SUN    SHADE ⬜ .

What I found:

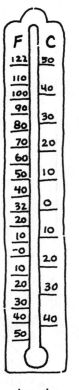  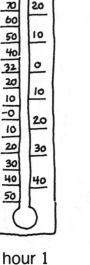 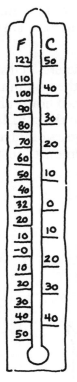  

begin   hour 1   hour 2   begin   hour 1   hour 2

I found the water in the   was hotter. (circle)

My conclusion is: _____

_____

A Cloudy Day

Concept: Clouds come in different shapes, sizes, and colors.

Materials: Magazine pictures showing puffy white cumulus clouds, wispy cirrus clouds, and black thunderhead clouds. *For each student:* cotton balls, construction paper, black and gray markers, glue, crayons.

Plan: Ask students to go to the window and to tell if they see any clouds in the sky. If they do, have them describe the clouds. Display the magazine pictures and have students describe the clouds in the pictures. Explain that clouds come in many shapes, sizes, and colors. Some clouds are big, white, and puffy; others are thin, wispy, and gray. Still others are big, puffy, and black. Ask students if they know what kind of weather big, puffy, black clouds might bring. Tell them that today they are going to make pictures with real clouds in them. Display a cloud picture that you have made to give students an idea of what they are to do. Help students brainstorm the kinds of clouds they can make. Remind them that they can make black and gray clouds by using the magic markers to color the cotton balls.

Distribute materials to students. Help them experiment with the cotton. Show them how to bunch up the cotton balls to make puffy clouds, how to stretch them out to make wispy clouds, and how to use markers to make rain or storm clouds. Suggest to students that they draw and color their pictures before gluing the clouds in place. Allow time for each student to present his or her picture to the class and to describe the weather he or she portrayed in the drawing. Display students' work on the bulletin board under the title "A Cloudy Day."

Cloud Formations

Concept: Clouds are classified according to their size, location, and color.

Materials: *For each group:* magazines, scissors, glue, poster board.
Additional Activity: hot plate, kettle, water, a spoon for each student.

Plan: Ask students to describe as many kinds of clouds as they can, and then tell them that clouds can be classified into three major groups: cirrus, cumulus, and stratus. On the chalkboard, draw examples of the three kinds of clouds as shown.

Cirrus   Cumulus   Stratus

Explain that cirrus clouds are the wispy, wavelike shapes high in the atmosphere. Cumulus clouds are the big puffy clouds that look like marshmallows (they may also be black thunderclouds). Cumulus clouds are usually found below cirrus clouds. Stratus clouds are thin layers of clouds found closest to the earth. Tell students they will work in groups to make charts showing the different kinds of clouds.

Distribute materials to each group with which to make a chart like the one shown. Have students look through magazines to find and cut out examples of each kind of cloud. Encourage students to discuss the category in which each cloud belongs before gluing it into place on the chart. Allow groups time to present their charts to the rest of the class.

Additional Activity: Make a Cloud

This activity is teacher-conducted because of the possible danger from steam and the heating element. Tell students that they are going to make a cloud in the classroom and that they might even produce a little rain. Explain that when water boils, steam escapes, and that steam is a cloud very similar to the clouds in the sky. Distribute a spoon to each student. Use the hot plate to bring the water in the kettle to a boil. Have students note the cloudlike water vapor that escapes. *Make sure that students are not too close to the kettle.* Have them hold their spoons toward the steam. The water vapor should condense on the spoon in the form of small droplets of water.

Predicting Weather

Concept: Clouds and temperature can be used to predict the weather.

Materials: Outdoor thermometer, activity sheet for each student (page 62).

Plan: Have students recall weather reports they have seen on television newscasts or have heard on the radio. Ask them how weather reports are helpful. Explain that a weather reporter must study many factors, such as temperature, air pressure, and humidity, before predicting the weather. Tell students that they will now have an opportunity to produce their own weather reports and that they will make their weather predictions by looking at the sky and by reading the temperature from an outdoor thermometer. Explain that the temperature will indicate whether the weather will be warm or cold, and, if the sky looks stormy, the temperature will also indicate whether it will rain or snow. Tell students that clouds, too, can be a clue as to whether or not there will be rain or snow. Copy the chart below onto the chalkboard.

Kind of Cloud	What It Means
Cirrus	first sign that rain or snow is on its way
Stratus	good chance of rain or snow
White cumulus	fair weather
Dark cumulus	stormy weather

Explain to students that cirrus clouds are the first sign that a storm might be approaching, stratus clouds also often bring rain or snow, and white cumulus clouds mean fair weather while gray or black ones mean stormy weather.

Set up a thermometer outside a classroom window. Then, with students working in groups of three, distribute the activity sheets. Have groups complete the activity sheets while preparing their weather reports. Assign one student in a group to report on the current weather and the rest of the day's forecast, one to offer advice on how to dress for the day, and the third to predict tomorrow's weather.

Allow groups time to rehearse their weather reports before presenting them to the class. You may wish to have a different group present the weather report each day.

Today's Forecast

Look at the sky. In the box, draw or write what you see.

The sun is   shining ☐   not shining ☐ .

There are clouds in the sky.   yes ☐   no ☐

What do these clouds tell you? _____

The temperature is _____ .   It is very cold ☐   cold ☐ .

very hot ☐   hot ☐ .

The rest of today's weather will be _____

_____ .

Later on today, it will   rain ☐   snow ☐   be sunny ☐   be cloudy ☐ .

How should people dress
for the weather today? _____

_____

_____

Tomorrow will be _____

_____

It will   rain ☐   snow ☐   be sunny ☐   be cloudy ☐ .

Measuring Rainfall

Concept: The amount of rain can be measured, recorded, and compared to rainfalls of previous years.

Materials: *For each group:* tall drinking glass that has the same diameter at the base as at the top, ruler, clear plastic tape.

Plan: Ask students to recall the last time it rained and to estimate how much rain fell. Write their responses on the chalkboard. Tell students that meteorologists (scientists who study weather) measure and record rainfall amounts in order to determine how much rain falls from one year to the next and whether one year is drier or wetter than another. Tell students that they will make a rain gauge to measure rainfall.

Have students work in groups and provide each group with materials. Tell students to make a rain gauge as shown in the diagram.

On the next rainy day, have groups place their rain gauges in different areas of the school grounds to see if their placement affects how much rain they collect. Toward the end of the day, have groups collect their gauges and record their findings on a chart such as the following.

Rainfall	
Date	Amount
Total	

Tell groups to keep their rainfall records for two weeks and then have them share and discuss their findings.

Rainbows

Concept: A rainbow occurs when the sun's light goes through raindrops in the air. Red, orange, yellow, green, blue, indigo, and violet are the colors in the rainbow.

Materials: Magazine picture of a rainbow, garden hose or water mister. *For each student:* drawing paper, crayons.

NOTE: This experiment will work only on a sunny day.

Plan: Display the magazine picture and ask students to describe the colors they see in the rainbow. Ask what color is at the top and which is at the bottom. Ask students to give their explanations of how rainbows form in the sky. Then tell them that light from the sun is made up of many colors that blend together to form a clear white light. Continue by explaining that when the light from the sun hits raindrops in the air, the light is broken down into its different colors, and a rainbow is produced. Tell students that today they are going to experiment with making their own rainbows.

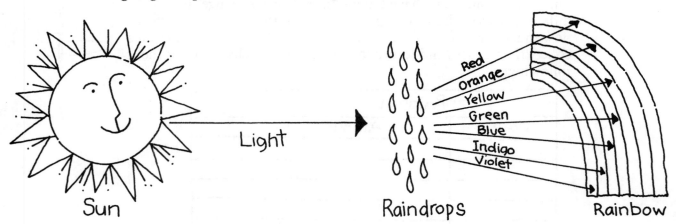

Take students outdoors and have them stand with their backs to the sun. Use the garden hose (or mister) to create a fine spray of water. Wait several seconds for a rainbow to appear. You may have to move the hose around or have students change their positions before the rainbow becomes visible. Once it is, tell students to observe the colors in the rainbow and the order in which they are arranged.

Discuss students' reactions and observations. Distribute drawing paper and crayons and have them draw their own rainbows. Display their drawings on the bulletin board.

Snowflakes

Concept: A snowflake is a six-sided crystal of ice.

Materials: *For each student:* black construction paper, magnifying glass, circles of white construction paper, string, scissors, magazine pictures that show falling snow.

NOTE: Is it best to do this activity at a time of year in which snow is likely to fall.

Plan: Ask students to think about the last time they saw snow and to describe what it was like. If you live in an area where snow does not fall, display the picture and ask students to imagine a snowfall. Explain that every snowflake that falls has six sides and will take one of seven basic shapes. Copy the shapes below on the chalkboard.

Tell students that the next time it snows they will have an opportunity to examine snowflakes. When the next snow does arrive, chill black construction paper by putting it outside the classroom window or in another place where it will be exposed to the cold. Then take students outdoors and give them the construction paper and magnifying glasses. Tell them to examine a snowflake with the magnifying glass as the flake falls on the black construction paper. Remind students to work quickly, for snowflakes melt rapidly.

Once they are back in the classroom, have students share their observations. Discuss whether they saw all seven of the basic snowflake shapes. Then tell them that they will have an opportunity to create their own snowflakes. Distribute several circles of white construction paper, scissors, and string to each student. Have them fold the paper as shown. Demonstrate how to cut designs on the sides of the paper and then unfold the paper to form a snowflake. Students' snowflakes may be hung with string in front of the classroom window.

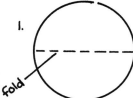 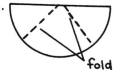

Additional Activity: How Deep Is the Snow?

Students who want to measure snowfall may make a snow gauge following the directions for the rain gauge on page 63.

Snow Pictures and Globes

Concept: Snowfalls may occur when the temperature reaches the freezing point. Snowfalls change the appearance of an area.

Materials: *For snow pictures:* construction paper, crayons, brushes, watered-down white glue, white cornmeal, newspapers. *For snow globes:* empty baby-food jars with lids, epoxy glue, white or silver glitter, small plastic figures (students may bring them from home), water.

Plan: Have students imagine that it is a very, very cold day and that they have to wear heavy clothes, jackets, scarves, hats, and gloves. Tell them that a big wind begins to blow and clouds fill the sky. Have them predict whether it will rain or snow. Explain that snow can occur when the temperature drops to the freezing point (32°F or 0°C). Help students to understand that when the temperature is above the freezing point, it will rain instead of snow. Tell them that today they will make pictures showing a snowfall. Spread newspapers on students' desks for protection. Then distribute crayons and construction paper to students and have them draw a picture showing a snowfall. Next, distribute brushes, glue, and cornmeal and demonstrate how to use a brush to apply glue to the areas of the picture where snow will appear. Continue by showing students how to sprinkle the cornmeal over the glue, moving the paper so that the cornmeal sticks to all areas of the paper containing glue. Shake excess cornmeal onto the newspaper. Now have students make their own snow pictures.

To make snow globes, have students bring in small plastic figures from home. Help them glue the figures upright on the inside of the lid from a baby-food jar. Allow time for the glue to dry. Tell students to fill the jar with water almost but not completely to the top and then to add a tablespoon of glitter. Have them carefully place the lid on the jar and *close tightly.* Students may then shake their jars and watch the "snow" fall.

The Four Seasons

Concept: There are four seasons that occur during the year: spring, summer, fall, and winter.

Materials: *For each student:* magazines, scissors, glue, index cards.

Plan: Write "summer," "fall," "winter," and "spring" on the chalkboard and ask students to discuss the activities they do during each season and to describe what the weather is like. Tell students that they are going to look through magazines to find and cut out pictures that show each season. As students cut out pictures, have them paste them on index cards. When they have finished, collect the index cards, shuffle them, and distribute an equal number to each student. Give students a moment to look at the cards and to identify the season depicted in each. Then tell them that they are going to play a game. Explain that you are going to describe a season. For example: It is a chilly, windy day. The red, gold, and brown leaves are falling from the trees. Children are raking leaves and picking apples (or any statement that is true for your region). Then all students who have a card showing that season should bring the card to the front of the room, display the picture to the rest of the class, and describe what the picture shows. Repeat this procedure with the other seasons.

After the game, display the cards on the bulletin board under the headings *Spring, Summer, Fall, Winter.*

Identifying Shapes

Concept: Solids take up space. Solids are different colors and shapes.

Materials: Several different color shapes such as sphere, block, rectangle, pyramid, cylinder; large box; an activity sheet for each student (page 69).

Plan: Place the shapes in a box. Call on a student to pick a shape and make up a sentence that tells about it. If necessary, help students by asking the following questions: "What shape is it? Is it big or small?" When all items have been chosen, tell students that they can find shapes or combinations of shapes all around them. Ask students to look around the classroom and identify the shapes they see.

Tell students that their own neighborhoods contain many different shapes. Go on a walk to see what different shapes they can find. As you walk, ask students to identify the various buildings and items that they see on the street. Ask students to describe the shapes. Are they square? Rectangular? Round? Triangular?

After the walk, allow students time to talk about the shapes they saw. Give each student an activity sheet and have them draw a picture of one shape they saw and write the name of the shape at the bottom of the sheet. Display students' work on the bulletin board.

Name _____   Date _____

Neighborhood Shapes

Shape: _____

Do Solids, Liquids, and Gases Take up Space?

Concept: Solids, liquids, and gases take up space. Liquids and most gases take the shape of their containers.

Materials: Several shapes, such as a sphere and a cube. *For each group:* water, ball of clay, paper cup, crayon, several different containers, balloon, activity sheet (page 71).

Plan: Place the sphere on a desk in front of you. Challenge students to put the cube in the same exact space the sphere occupies. Then ask them why they cannot do this. Tell students that today they will conduct experiments to see if solids, liquids, and gases take up space.

Have students work in groups and distribute materials to each group. Ask groups to make their predictions on the activity sheets and then to follow the procedure for each experiment as indicated below.

Do solids take up space? Tell groups to fill the cup half full of water and to mark the water line with a crayon. Next have them mush up the clay so that there are no air holes, drop the clay into the water, and mark the line of the water. Tell groups to remove the clay without spilling any water. Have them form the clay into another shape and drop it into the cup again. Tell groups to record their findings on the activity sheet.

Do liquids take up space? Have groups pour water into a container. Then have them add more water. Have them record their findings on the activity sheet.

Do gases take up space? Have groups take a balloon and stretch it. Then help them partially blow up the balloon and tie a knot in it. Ask students to try to put the balloon in their pocket. Have them record their observations on their activity sheets.

Allow groups time to share their observations with the rest of the class. Help students draw conclusions about whether solids, liquids, and gases take up space.

Name _____ Date _____

Do Solids, Liquids, and Gases Take up Space?

Do solids take up space?

We predict: yes ☐   no ☐

What we found:_____

_____

_____

Do liquids take up space?

We predict: yes ☐   no ☐

What we found:_____

_____

_____

Do gases take up space?

We predict: yes ☐   no ☐

What we found:_____

_____

_____

Our conclusions:_____

_____

_____

_____

Can a Liquid Change to a Gas and Can a Gas Change to a Liquid?

Concept: A liquid can change to a gas. A gas can change to a liquid.

Materials: Water, measuring cup, hot plate, kettle, saucepan lid, pot holder, activity sheet (page 73) for each student.

Plan: Ask students to tell whether or not they think a liquid can become a gas and a gas can become a liquid. Tell them that today they will conduct an experiment to see if such changes can happen. (Because of the potential danger involved in working with boiling water, this activity is teacher-conducted.)

Distribute activity sheets to students and have them make their first prediction. Have a volunteer measure 1 cup (250 ml) of water and pour it into the kettle. Bring the water to a boil. Remove the kettle lid. Allow students to take turns observing the boiling water at a safe distance and have them record their observations.

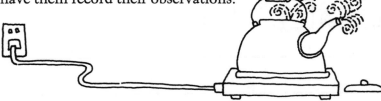

After about five minutes, remove the kettle from the hot plate and allow the water to cool. Then pour the water into the measuring cup and have students note the water level. Ask them why there is less water now than before. Discuss students' responses.

Now direct students to the second part of the experiment. Have them make their predictions on the activity sheet. Pour 1 cup (250 ml) of water into the kettle and bring it to a boil. As the steam escapes the kettle, use a pot holder to hold the saucepan lid a few inches (cm) from the kettle spout. Allow students to take turns observing the moisture on the lid.

When they have recorded their observations, ask them where they think the water drops on the lid came from. Discuss their responses. Then help students draw conclusions based on their observations.

Liquid to Gas? Gas to Liquid?

Can a liquid change to a gas?

I predict: yes ☐   no ☐

What I found:_____

_____

_____

_____

Can a gas change to a liquid?

I predict: yes ☐   no ☐

What I found:_____

_____

_____

_____

My conclusions:_____

_____

_____

_____

What Colors Make up White Light?

Concept: White light is made up of red, orange, yellow, green, blue, and purple.

Materials: Prism. *For each student:* red, orange, green, blue, yellow, and purple crayons; small circle of white paper (3-inch/ 7½-cm diameter); straight pin; pencil with eraser.

Plan: Have students answer this question: What color is white light? After writing their responses on the chalkboard, display the prism. Explain that a prism will break up white light into the colors that make up the light. Have students take turns looking through the prism. When they are finished, ask volunteers to name the colors they saw and write their observations on the chalkboard.

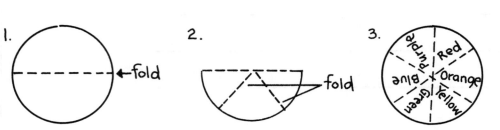

Tell students they will now conduct their own experiment to prove that white light is made up of red, orange, yellow, green, blue, and purple. Distribute crayons and a circle to each student. Have students fold the circle as shown below.

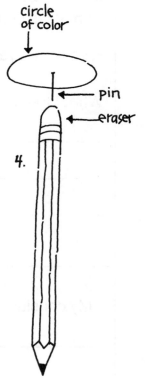

Then have them unfold the circle and color the six sections red, orange, yellow, green, blue, and purple (one color per section).

Help students use the pin to attach the color wheel to the eraser of the pencil.

Then demonstrate how to roll the pencil very rapidly between the palms of the hands. Allow students time to try this and to observe what happens. They should be able to see the six colors blend to make white. Have students share their observations and conclusions.

Exploring the Properties of Color

Concept: When two colors are mixed together, they make a different color.

Materials: Magazine picture showing several primary colors. *For each pair of students:* red, yellow, and blue tempera; small paper cups; water; plastic spoons; paintbrushes; white drawing paper; color chart.

Color Chart

We mixed		We got
[ ] ✚ [ ]		[ ]
[ ] ✚ [ ]		[ ]
[ ] ✚ [ ]		[ ]

Mix 3 colors together. What color do you get?

[ ] ✚ [ ] ✚ [ ] = [ ]

Plan: Display the magazine picture and have students name the colors they see. Write their responses on the chalkboard. Then display the jars of red, yellow, and blue paint. Tell students that they are going to try mixing colors to make other colors.

Have students work in pairs and distribute materials and a color chart to each pair. Tell students to mix two different colors to see what new color they get. As they experiment, they are to note on their color charts the two colors they mixed and the color that resulted. Demonstrate how to take small amounts of paint and to mix them in a clean paper cup. (Remind students to wash spoons thoroughly with water after each experiment.) Ask students to suggest some possible color combinations and write their suggestions on the chalkboard (red/yellow, red/blue, yellow/blue). After pairs have completed their experiments, allow them to compare their findings with classmates.

Distribute drawing paper and brushes to students to use with their paints to create pictures for display on the classroom bulletin board.

Changing the Properties of Matter

Concept: The properties of matter can be changed.

Materials: *For each student:* powdered laundry detergent, food coloring, small paper cup, water, plastic spoon.

Plan: Display the laundry detergent and ask students what some of its uses are. Explain that in addition to being used to clean soiled clothing, detergent has other uses. Tell students they are going to make crayons with laundry detergent.

Provide each student with a paper cup and a plastic spoon and fill each cup almost to the top with detergent. Have students add a small amount of water and mix well. Distribute small bottles of different food coloring to students, telling them to add thirty drops of one color to their cups and to stir well. Put the detergent mixture in a warm place for three or four days or until the water has evaporated. Then have students remove the paper cup and examine their crayons made out of laundry detergent.

1. Fill to here with laundry detergent.

2. Add a small amount of water. Stir.

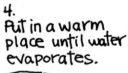

3. Add thirty drops of food coloring and stir.

4. Put in a warm place until water evaporates.

5. Peel off paper cup.

Allow students to color any nonporous surface with the crayon and then to wipe the surface clean with a wet rag. (Check to see if a surface is usable before allowing students to color.) Give students time to share their observations.

Experimenting with Planes

Concept: A plane is a simple machine that can make work easier.

Materials: 4-foot-long (1¼-m) small board, heavy book. *For each group:* large piece of cardboard, poster board strips, masking tape, cups, paper towel tubes, scissors, marbles, paper clips.

Plan: Call for two volunteers to come to the front of the room and tell one to sit on the floor. Ask the volunteer who is standing to pass a heavy book to the seated volunteer. Then take the board and ask the volunteer who is standing to hold it at an angle and to slide the book down to the seated student. Ask students which task required less work. Explain that the board is a slide, or plane, and that a plane is a simple machine that can make work easier. Tell students that today they will experiment with planes.

Have students work in groups and distribute materials to each group. Tell groups you want them to design obstacle courses for the marbles. Display the following to students to give them an idea of what they are to do.

Tell groups to use the cardboard as bases for their courses and to roll and tape the poster board to form tubes. Provide help as necessary. When students have finished, they may experiment with how the marbles move along the courses. Encourage them to experiment also with paper clips.

Allow groups time to demonstrate their courses. Students may discuss which course is fastest and give their reasons for why this may be so. Ask students to identify ways in which planes or slides are useful to us in our everyday lives.

Experimenting with Levers

Concept: A lever is a simple machine that can make work easier.

Materials: *For each pair of students:* two pencils, heavy book, construction paper, crayons.

Plan: Have students work in pairs. Make sure each pair has two pencils and a heavy book. Tell them to place the book on the desk and to use the pencils to lift the book. After students have had some time to experiment, ask pairs who were successful to demonstrate for the rest of the class. If students have not been able to demonstrate the principle of the lever, do so for them now. Have pairs practice using the pencils as levers.

Explain to students that a lever is a simple machine that makes it easier to do work. Tell them that today they are going to make pictures that show people using levers to help them do work.

Before beginning, help students brainstorm the kinds of work for which people might use a lever: to lift a heavy rock, to pry open the top of a heavy crate, to take the lid off a paint can. Then distribute the construction paper and crayons and have students draw their pictures. Display students' pictures on the classroom bulletin board or bind them in a class book entitled *Levers at Work.*

Do Wheels Make Work Easier?

Concept: Wheels can make work easier.

Materials: *For each group:* two wooden blocks, four large plastic bottle tops or lids, four nails.

NOTE: Before you begin this activity, attach wheels to one of the blocks by making a hole in the top of each bottle cap. Nail the bottle cap "wheels" to each block. Turn the wheels until they spin easily. Prepare one block with wheels for each group in your classroom.

Plan: Have students imagine two sisters who live in the same house and who are on their way to school. One sister will ride her bike to school, and the other will walk. Ask students which sister will get to school first and why. Most students will say that the sister who rides a bike will get there first because riding a bicycle is faster than walking. Tell them that today they will conduct an experiment to discover if wheels help make work, such as walking, easier.

Have students work in groups and distribute materials. Tell each of the group members to push the block without wheels across the floor and to note how easily the block moves. Then tell them to do the same thing with the block that has wheels.

Allow groups to discuss their observations and to draw conclusions.

Machines at Work

Concept: Many machines are at work in the neighborhood.

Materials: *For each student:* crayons, activity sheet (page 81). *For Additional Activity: For each student:* construction paper, crayons.

Plan: Tell students that many different kinds of machines are at work right in their own neighborhood. Call on volunteers to name some of these machines. Tell students that they will take a walk in the neighborhood to find machines at work.

As you walk with students, help them identify the various machines they see and whether they use wheels, levers, planes, or a combination of these simple machines.

Back in the classroom, allow students to talk about the machines they saw. Write their responses on the chalkboard and distribute crayons and activity sheets. Tell students to draw on their activity sheets a picture of one machine they saw on their walk. Ask them to write "plane," "lever," or "wheels" at the bottom of their drawing. Allow each student to present his or her drawing to the class and to tell about the kind of work the machine does. Students' work may be displayed on the bulletin board under the title "Machines at Work."

Additional Activity: Crazy Machines!

Ask students to think about a silly machine they might invent. It might be a fancy toy, a homework machine, or a machine that ties shoelaces. Have them think about what device their machines would have—lever, plane, or wheels, or a combination of these. Distribute construction paper and crayons and have students draw their machines. Allow students to present their machines to the rest of the class. Encourage them to describe what the machine does and to explain how it works.

Machines in Our Neighborhood

Kind of machine: _____

Exploring Night and Day

Concept: Light is a form of energy that helps people to see.

Materials: *For each student:* white construction paper, crayons, paintbrushes, watered-down black tempera, newspaper.

Plan: Call on students to describe various outdoor areas in their neighborhood, such as the park, school playground, street on which they live, and ask them to name the activities that go on in these areas during the day. Write their responses on the chalkboard. Then ask them if the same activities that occur during the day occur at night. Discuss with students how, during the day, energy in the form of sunlight allows them to see and therefore to be able to do things. Explain that since at night there is no sunlight, they are unable to see well enough to do the activities they do during the day. Ask students what they use at night in order to be able to see.

Tell students that today they will make pictures of places during the day and during the night. Distribute white construction paper and crayons to students. Tell them to choose a place in the neighborhood and to draw *two* pictures of it. Have them try to make the pictures identical. Tell students to color in completely all shapes in their pictures, not just outline them. If students have trouble coming up with ideas for their pictures, suggest scenes such as the block on which they live, including houses, apartment buildings, and the like and the main street of their neighborhood, showing stores and/or office buildings. Have students label one picture "Day" and the other picture "Night."

Then cover the desks with newspaper for protection. Distribute brushes and watered-down black tempera. Tell students to paint over their "Night" pictures with the black paint. Allow time for the paint to dry. All the space that was not colored with crayon will be dark in this picture. Give students time to examine their pictures and to talk about how daytime and nighttime differ. Display students' pictures on the bulletin board.

Exploring Light and Shadows

Concept: Shadows are created when an object blocks a light source.

Materials: Bright light, large piece of white construction paper. *For each group:* popsicle sticks, shadow play cutouts (see page 84), heavy construction paper, pencils, scissors, tape.

Plan: Hang the construction paper on the wall and shine the bright light on it. Have students note that the light is shining directly on the paper and that nothing is blocking it. Hold your hand in front of the light so that it casts a shadow on the paper. Ask students why they think the shadow of your hand is now on the paper. Help them to see that your hand is blocking the light.

Help students to make the shadow figures. They will enjoy experimenting with the light to make shadows of birds, rabbits, and dinosaurs.

rabbit   dinosaur   bird

Then tell students they will work in groups to adapt a story they know for presentation as a shadow play. Explain that in their plays they will use the shadow figures along with figures they will cut out from construction paper. Duplicate and distribute the shadow-play figures as well as other materials. Instruct students to cut out the figures, trace them onto heavy construction paper, cut out the figures once again, and tape them to craft sticks. Help students adapt existing cutouts to make characters specific to their stories.

Provide time for students to practice their plays before performing them for the class.

Shadow Play Cutouts

Escaping Heat

Concept: Energy can be lost through doors and windows that are not properly insulated.

Materials: *For each student:* 8-inch (20-cm) length of ribbon, activity sheet (page 86).
NOTE: A similar experiment may be conducted with students who live in warm climates. These students may check to see if cold air is escaping through doorways and windows.

Plan: Ask students to imagine that it is a very cold day and then have them tell how they keep warm on such a day. Point out to students that wearing layers of clothing is a good way to insulate the body and keep it warm. Explain that houses have insulation, too, and that the insulation helps to keep houses warm during cold weather. Ask students what would happen if, on a very cold day, a window in a house were left open.

After explaining that "leaks" around windows and doors can cause heat to escape, tell students that they will conduct individual surveys of their homes to discover if heat is escaping through doors and windows. Provide each student with an activity sheet (see page 86) and a length of ribbon. Have students conduct their surveys on a cold, windy day. Instruct them to follow these procedures:

■ Hold the ribbon up around windows and doors. Keep your hand still.
■ Does the ribbon move? If so, you have found a leak. On your activity sheet, draw a diagram showing the location of the leak.

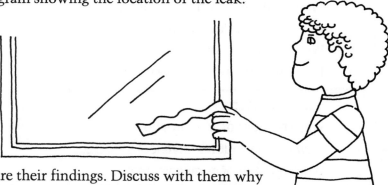

Provide students time to share their findings. Discuss with them why identifying and fixing leaks is important and have them brainstorm ways of fixing leaks. You may suggest caulking windows, covering windows with plastic sheeting, using insulation tape to stop leaks in doorways, and so on. Encourage students to share their findings with their families.

Students who wish to do so may conduct the same type of survey in the classroom.

Name _____ Date _____

Is Heat Escaping?

Check doors leading to the outside.   Is heat escaping?

Front door   ☐ yes   ☐ no

Back door   ☐ yes   ☐ no

Cellar door   ☐ yes   ☐ no

Door leading to the garage   ☐ yes   ☐ no

Other doors   ☐ yes   ☐ no

Kitchen

Write number of windows here. _____

How many windows have leaks? _____

Write number of doorways here. _____

How many doorways have leaks? _____

Draw a diagram here showing location of the leaks.

Living Room

Write number of windows here. _____

How many windows have leaks? _____

Write number of doorways here. _____

How many doorways have leaks? _____

Draw a diagram here showing location of the leaks.

_____'s Bedroom

Write number of windows here. _____

How many windows have leaks? _____

Write number of doorways here. _____

How many doorways have leaks? _____

Draw a diagram here showing location of the leaks.

_____'s Bedroom

Write number of windows here. _____

How many windows have leaks? _____

Write number of doorways here. _____

How many doorways have leaks? _____

Draw a diagram here showing location of the leaks.

_____ room

Write number of windows here. _____

How many windows have leaks? _____

Write number of doorways here. _____

How many doorways have leaks? _____

Draw a diagram here showing location of the leaks.

How Can Water Be Kept Warm?

Concept: Covering a bowl of hot water can prevent heat loss.

Materials: *For each group:* two 8-ounce (250-ml) glass jars, very hot tap water, thermometer, aluminum pie tin. *For each student:* recording sheet.
NOTE: Caution students to handle the hot water carefully.

Plan: Have students imagine that they have just cooked a pot of soup. Ask them how they could keep the soup warm without reheating it and write their responses on the chalkboard. Tell students that today they will conduct an experiment to see how they might keep a liquid warm. Have students work in groups. Write the following recording sheet on the chalkboard and have each student copy it.

How Can Water Be Kept Warm?
I predict . . .
Water can be kept warm ☐ with a lid   ☐ without a lid

Temperature of water in jar #1 _____   Temperature of water in jar #2 _____

After five minutes   Temperature of water in jar #1 _____
                                          Temperature of water in jar #2 _____

My conclusions: _____
_____

Have students conduct the experiment under your supervision. Tell them to follow these steps:

- Label the jars #1 and #2. Make predictions.
- Carefully fill each jar with hot water. Fill each jar to the same level.
- Use the thermometer to record the temperature in each jar.
- Remove the thermometer and let it cool down. Place the pie tin over the top of jar #1.
- Wait five minutes. Then use the thermometer to record the temperature in each jar (place the thermometer in cool water in between recordings) and record findings.

When the experiment is over, have groups draw conclusions and share their observations.

Sound Travels Through Different Materials

Concept: Sound can travel through different materials.

Materials: *For each group:* large glass jar, water, sponge, book, piece of wood, marbles, pencils; activity sheet for each student (page 89).

Plan: Discuss with students how they are able to hear the noises and voices around them. Explain that when people talk, the sound travels through the air and is picked up by the ear. Ask students if they think sound travels through other materials such as glass, water, wood, and so on, and write their responses on the chalkboard. Then tap a pencil against the wall. Ask students if the sound they heard traveled through the air. Then have several students place one ear against a wall and use a hand to cover the other ear. Tap the pencil against the wall and ask students if the noise sounded the same as when you did it before. Tell students that today they will experiment to discover if sound travels through different materials.

Have students work in groups and distribute materials. Give each student an activity sheet and instruct the class to proceed as follows:

- Fill the jar with water. The group listens as one student taps two marbles together. Then students take turns putting an ear against the side of the jar as a student taps marbles together under the water.
- The group listens as one student taps two pencils together. Then students take turns putting a sponge next to their ear and listening as the two pencils are tapped together next to the sponge.
- The group listens as one student taps two pencils together. Then students take turns putting a block of wood next to their ear and listening as the two pencils are tapped together next to the wood.
- The group listens as one student taps two marbles together. Then students take turns holding a book next to their ear and listening as the two marbles are tapped together next to the book.

Allow groups time to share their findings and observations with the class.

Sound Travels Through Many Materials

Listen.

How did it sound?

Listen.

How did it sound?

Listen.

How did it sound?

Listen.

How did it sound?

Listen.

How did it sound?

Listen.

How did it sound?

Listen.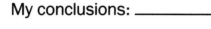

How did it sound?

Listen.

How did it sound?

My conclusions: _____

_____

_____

_____

Recognizing Different Sounds

Concept: Sounds can be useful to humans.

Materials: Homemade audiotape of fifteen to twenty different sounds, such as telephone ringing, car horn honking, smoke detector, doorbell, school guard whistle, school bell, car alarm, tricycle bell, dog barking, fire engine or police siren, ambulance siren. *For each student:* crayons and drawing paper.

Plan: Ask students to think of different sounds and how they might be helpful to us. Begin by mentioning an alarm clock and asking students how an alarm clock is useful. Write students' suggestions on the chalkboard. Next, tell students that they will listen to a tape. Explain that as each sound is played, they are to identify the sound and describe how the sound is helpful.

Distribute drawing paper and crayons to students. Have each student choose one item heard on the tape. Tell students to draw and color a picture illustrating how the sound is helpful to people. Use the drawings to create a bulletin board display entitled "How Sounds Help Us."

Additional Activity: How Many Sounds?

Take students on a fifteen-minute walk through the neighborhood. As they walk, have them note all the different sounds they hear. On returning to the classroom, have students categorize the sounds they heard. Some categories might be "Helpful Sounds," "Sound Pollution," "Other Sounds."

How Can Sound Pollution Be Reduced?

Concept: Insulation can reduce sound pollution.

Materials: *For each group:* clock with a loud tick, shoe box with cover, fabric scraps, newspaper. *For each student:* recording sheet.

Plan: Ask students if they have ever heard a particularly irritating noise that they wished would stop. Ask them what they did to reduce the noise and write their responses on the chalkboard. Discuss with students the problem of sound pollution in the environment. Tell them that today they will conduct an experiment to discover if sound pollution can be reduced.

Have students work in groups. Write the following recording sheet on the chalkboard and have students copy it.

Can Sound Pollution Be Reduced?

I predict ☐ yes ☐ no

How the clock sounded at the beginning of the experiment:

_____

How the clock sounded at the end of the experiment:_____

_____

My conclusion:_____

_____

Tell students to:

- Record their predictions.
- Place the clock in the shoe box and put on the cover.
- Place their ears against the side of the shoe box and listen. Record the noise they hear.
- Use fabric scraps and newspaper to insulate the inside of the box. Return the clock to the box and listen again. Record the noise they hear.
- Discuss observations with the group and draw conclusions.
- Allow groups time to discuss and share their findings.

Electrical Safety

Concept: Improper use of electrical appliances can be extremely dangerous.

Materials: Electric hair dryer. *For each student:* drawing paper, crayons.

Plan: Plug in the electric hair dryer and turn it on for a few seconds. Turn off the dryer but leave it plugged in. Ask students what powered the dryer. Discuss how electricity is a powerful energy source that makes it possible to light houses and streets, run machinery, refrigerate food, and do many other things. Explain that electricity can also be dangerous, especially if it is used improperly. Point out that although the hair dryer is off, it is still plugged in and therefore a current of electricity still runs through the wires. Explain that if a person holding the hair dryer were accidentally to come into contact with water, he or she could get a severe electric shock. Emphasize that for this reason electrical appliances should not be used near water.

Work with students to formulate rules to follow when using electrical appliances. As students state a rule, write it on the chalkboard. You may want to suggest some of the following rules to help students get started:

- Make sure the iron is turned off and unplugged after using.
- Do not use a hair dryer or any other electrical appliance while taking a bath.
- Keep small children away from appliances and electrical outlets.
- If there is a small child in the house, fit electrical outlets with childproof plugs.
- If you use an extension cord, make sure the cord can carry the same wattage as the appliance.
- Do not overload outlets with too many appliances.
- Mend frayed wires on appliances.

Invite each student to make a poster illustrating one of the rules. Display posters in the school corridors under the title "Electrical Safety."

Suggest to students that they and a parent survey their homes to locate possible electrical safety hazards. After giving students several days to conduct their surveys, allow time for them to share their findings with the class.

What Is a Magnet? How Does It Work?

Concept: A magnet is a stone or piece of iron or steel that attracts or draws to it other bits of iron or steel. A compass needle will point to the north magnetic pole.

Materials: Several magnets (including at least one bar magnet); metal objects, such as paper clips; a compass. *For each group:* plastic bowl, water, cork about 1/2 inch (1 1/4 cm) thick, compass needles (see Note), red nail polish.

NOTE: Prepare the compass needles beforehand. Use a scissor to cut them from the lid of a tin can (not aluminum).

Plan: Ask students if their families use their refrigerators at home to display drawings or to post messages. Have students tell how the drawings and messages are kept in place. Discuss magnets with students. Tell them that a magnet attracts metal, and for this reason it "sticks" to the refrigerator. Display a magnet and demonstrate how metal objects are attracted to it. Allow students time to experiment with magnets.

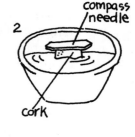
bar magnet

compass needle

Then tell students that magnets can help people find their way. Display a compass. Tell students that the small needle is magnetized and will always point to the North because of a large magnetic area that exists very near to the North Pole. Explain that just as the metal objects are attracted to the magnet, so the needle is attracted to this magnetic area. Point out that if a person wanted to walk north he or she would look at the compass and follow the needle. Allow students time to hold the compass and to notice how the needle always points to the North.

compass needle

cork

Tell students they will work in groups to complete the steps necessary to make their own compasses. Distribute materials.

1. Have students magnetize the needle by stroking it in one direction *only* with the bar magnet.
2. Tell them to place the cork in a bowl 2/3 filled with water and then to place the compass needle on the cork.
3. Have students observe which end points north (students may want to use the compass to determine north). Tell students to put a bit of red nail polish on the end pointing north.

nail polish

Encourage groups to test their compasses by moving the bowl around to determine if the needle always points north. Allow groups time to share their thoughts and findings.

Bibliography

Pages 7–30

Adler, David A. *Redwoods Are the Tallest Trees in the World* Crowell, 1978.
Adoff, Arnold *Friend Dog* Lippincott, 1980.
Aliki *Corn Is Maize, The Gift of the Indians* Harper, 1976.
Brandt, Keith *Discovering Trees* Troll, 1982.
Carlstrom, Nancy White *Moose in the Garden* Harper, 1990.
Cole, Joanna *Plants in Winter* Crowell, 1973.
Curran, Eileen *Birds' Nests* Troll, 1985.
         Life in the Forest Troll, 1985.
         Life in the Meadow Troll,1985.
         Life in the Pond Troll, 1985.
         Life in the Sea Troll, 1985.
         Look at a Tree Troll, 1985.
Dorros, Arthur *Ant Cities* Harper, 1987.
Dowden, Anne Ophelia *The Clover & the Bee: A Book of Pollination* Harper, 1990.
Dr. Seuss *Horton Hatches the Egg* Random House, 1940.
Eastman, David *What Is a Fish?* Troll, 1982.
Ferguson, Alane *That New Pet!* Lothrop, Lee and Shepard, 1986.
Gordon, Sharon *Dolphins and Porpoises* Troll, 1985.
         Trees Troll, 1982.
Jacobs, Leland B. *Poems about Fur and Feather Friends* Garrard, 1971.
Jordan, Helene J. *How a Seed Grows* Crowell, 1960.
Keats, Ezra Jack *Clementina's Cactus* Viking, 1982.
Kuchalla, Susan *What Is a Reptile?* Troll, 1982.
Lasky, Kathryn *Sugaring Time* Macmillan, 1983.
Lauber, Patricia *Snakes Are Hunters* Harper, 1989.
Lavies, Bianca *Tree Trunk Traffic* Dutton, 1989.
Lobel, Arnold *Grasshopper on the Road* Harper, 1978.
McCloskey, Robert *Blueberries for Sal* Viking, 1948.
Provensen, Alice and Martin *Town and Country* Crown, 1985.
Sabin, Louis *Amazing World of Butterflies and Moths* Troll, 1982.
Selsam, Millicent E. *More Potatoes!* Harper, 1972.
Sendak, Maurice, and Matthew Margolis *Some Swell Pup or Are You Sure You Want a Dog?* Farrar, Straus, 1976.
Watson, Clyde *Applebet: An ABC* Farrar, Straus, 1982.
Whipple, Laura, Comp. *Eric Carle's Animals, Animals* Philomel, 1990.
Williams, John *The Life Cycle of a Tree* Bookwright, 1989.
Yoshida, Toshi *Young Lions* Philomel, 1989.

Pages 31–42

Aliki *My Five Senses* Crowell, 1989.

Carlstrom, Nancy White *Wild Wild Sunflower Child Anna*
Macmillan, 1987.

Cobb, Vicki *Keeping Clean* Lippincott, 1989.

Cole, Joanna *Cuts, Breaks, Bruises, and Burns: How Your Body Heals*
Crowell, 1985.

Garelick, May *Just My Size* Harper, 1990.

Harshman, Terry Webb *Porcupine's Pajama Party* Harper, 1990.

Hutchins, Pat *You'll Soon Grow into Them, Titch* Greenwillow, 1985.

Korschunow, Irina *Small Fur Is Getting Bigger.* Translated by James
Skofield Harper, 1990.

Kuskin, Karla *The Philharmonic Gets Dressed* Harper, 1982.

Martin, Bill, and H. John Archambault *Here Are My Hands* Holt, 1989.

McNamara, Louise G., and Ada B. Litchfield *Your Living Bones*
Little, Brown, 1973.

Nerlove, Miriam *Just One Tooth* McElderry, 1989.

Showers, Paul *A Drop of Blood* Crowell, 1989.
Ears Are for Hearing Crowell, 1990.
You Can't Make a Move Without Your Muscles
Crowell, 1982.

Smith, Kathie Billingslea and Crenson, Victoria *Hearing* Troll, 1987.
Seeing Troll, 1987.
Smelling Troll, 1987.
Tasting Troll, 1987.
Touching Troll, 1987.

Sonnenschein, Harriet *Harold's Runaway Nose* Simon & Schuster, 1989.

Waddell, Martin *Once There Were Giants* Delacorte, 1989.

West, Collin *The King's Toothache* Harper, 1990.

Zolotow, Charlotte *I Like to Be Little* Harper, 1987.

Pages 43–67

Aardema, Verna *Bringing the Rain to Kapiti Plain. A Nandi Tale*
Dial, 1981.

Barrett, Judi *Cloudy with a Chance of Meatballs* Atheneum, 1978.

Bartlett, Margaret *Where Does All the Rain Go?* Coward, 1973.

Bassett, Preston R., with Margaret Farrington Bartlett *Raindrop Stories*
Four Winds, 1981.

Baylor, Byrd *The Desert Is Theirs* Scribners, 1975.

Brandt, Keith *Wonders of the Seasons* Troll, 1982.

Branley, Franklyn M. *Flash, Crash, Rumble, and Roll* Harper, 1985.

Briggs, Raymond *The Snowman* Random House, 1978.

Burningham, John *Mr. Gumpy's Outing* Holt, 1971.

Curran, Eileen *Mountains and Volcanoes* Troll, 1985.

Dineen, Jacqueline *Let's Look At Rain* Brookwright, 1989.

Gans, Roma *Rock Collecting* Crowell, 1984.

Hopkins, Lee Bennett *The Sky Is Full of Song* Harper, 1983.

Johnson, Crockett *Will Spring Be Early? Or Will Spring Be Late?*
Harper, 1990.

Keats, Ezra Jack *The Snowy Day* Puffin, 1976.

Lauber, Patricia *How We Learned the Earth Is Round* Harper, 1990.

Livingston, Myra Cohn *A Circle of Seasons* Holiday House, 1982.

McNulty, Faith *How to Dig a Hole to the Other Side of the World*
    Harper, 1979.

Milburn, Constance *Let's Look at the Seasons* Bookwright, 1988.

Orlowsky, Wallace and Thomas B. Perera
    Who Will Clean the Air? Coward McCann, 1971.
    Who Will Wash the River? Coward McCann, 1970

Palazzo, Janet *What Makes the Weather* Troll, 1982.

Prelutsky, Jack *It's Snowing! It's Snowing!* Greenwillow, 1984.

Pringle, Laurence *Twist, Wiggle, and Squirm: A Book About
    Earthworms* Crowell, 1973.

Quackenbush, Robert *Calling Dr. Quack* Lothrop, Lee, and Shepard, 1978.

Santrey, Laurence *What Makes the Wind?* Troll, 1982.

Simon, Seymour *Earth: Our Planet in Space* Four Winds, 1984.

Skofield, James *All Wet! All Wet!* Harper, 1984.

Stevens, Carla *Anna, Grandpa, and the Big Storm* Clarion, 1982.

Stolz, Mary *Storm in the Night* Harper, 1990.

Wandelmaier, Roy *Clouds* Troll, 1985.

Pages 68–93

Balestrino, Phillip *Hot as an Ice Cube* Crowell, 1971.

Berenstain, Stan and Jan *Bears on Wheels* Random House, 1969.

Berger, Melvin *Switch On, Switch Off* Harper, 1989.

Burningham, John *Mr. Gumpy's Motor Car* Holt, 1976.

Calhoun, Mary *Hot-Air Henry* Morrow, 1981.

Coerr, Eleanor *The Big Balloon Race* Harper, 1981.
                The Mixed-Up Mystery Smell Putnam, 1976.

Cole, Joanna *It's Too Noisy!* Crowell, 1989.

Couture, Susan Arkin *The Block Book* Harper, 1990.

Crews, Donald *Harbor* Greenwillow, 1982.

Ehlert, Lois *Color Farm* Harper, 1990.

Fleischman, Paul *Shadow Play* Harper, 1990.

Goffstein, Brooke *A House, A Home* Harper, 1989.

Holabird, Katharine *Angelina Ballerina* Crown, 1983.

Hopkins, Lee Bennett, ed. *Click, Rumble, Roar: Poems About
    Machines* Crowell, 1987.

Kirkpatrick, Rena K. *Look at Magnets* Raintree, 1985.

Kuskin, Karla *Roar and More* Harper, 1990.

Mahy, Margaret *The Boy with Two Shadows* Lippincott, 1988.

Marquardt, Max *Wilbur, Orville, and the Flying Machine* Raintree, 1989.

Scarry, Richard *Richard Scarry's Cars and Trucks and Things That Go* Western, 1974.

Seibert, Diane *Train Song* Harper, 1990.

Seixas, Judith S. *Water—What It Is, What It Does* Greenwillow, 1987.

Walsh, Ellen Stoll *Mouse Paint* Harcourt, 1989.

Westcott, Nadine Bernard *There's a Hole in the Bucket* Harper, 1990.

Carlstrom, Nancy White *Wild Wild Sunflower Child Anna*
  Macmillan, 1987.
Cobb, Vicki *Keeping Clean* Lippincott, 1989.
Cole, Joanna *Cuts, Breaks, Bruises, and Burns: How Your Body Heals*
  Crowell, 1985.
Garelick, May *Just My Size* Harper, 1990.
Harshman, Terry Webb *Porcupine's Pajama Party* Harper, 1990.
Hutchins, Pat *You'll Soon Grow into Them, Titch* Greenwillow, 1985.
Korschunow, Irina *Small Fur Is Getting Bigger.* Translated by James
  Skofield Harper, 1990.
Kuskin, Karla *The Philharmonic Gets Dressed* Harper, 1982.
Martin, Bill, and H. John Archambault *Here Are My Hands* Holt, 1989.
McNamara, Louise G., and Ada B. Litchfield *Your Living Bones*
  Little, Brown, 1973.
Nerlove, Miriam *Just One Tooth* McElderry, 1989.
Showers, Paul *A Drop of Blood* Crowell, 1989.
              Ears Are for Hearing Crowell, 1990.
              You Can't Make a Move Without Your Muscles
              Crowell, 1982.
Smith, Kathie Billingslea and Crenson, Victoria *Hearing* Troll, 1987.
                                                  Seeing Troll, 1987.
                                                  Smelling Troll, 1987.
                                                  Tasting Troll, 1987.
                                                  Touching Troll, 1987.
Sonnenschein, Harriet *Harold's Runaway Nose* Simon & Schuster, 1989.
Waddell, Martin *Once There Were Giants* Delacorte, 1989.
West, Collin *The King's Toothache* Harper, 1990.
Zolotow, Charlotte *I Like to Be Little* Harper, 1987.

Pages 43–67

Aardema, Verna *Bringing the Rain to Kapiti Plain. A Nandi Tale*
  Dial, 1981.
Barrett, Judi *Cloudy with a Chance of Meatballs* Atheneum, 1978.
Bartlett, Margaret *Where Does All the Rain Go?* Coward, 1973.
Bassett, Preston R., with Margaret Farrington Bartlett *Raindrop Stories*
  Four Winds, 1981.
Baylor, Byrd *The Desert Is Theirs* Scribners, 1975.
Brandt, Keith *Wonders of the Seasons* Troll, 1982.
Branley, Franklyn M. *Flash, Crash, Rumble, and Roll* Harper, 1985.
Briggs, Raymond *The Snowman* Random House, 1978.
Burningham, John *Mr. Gumpy's Outing* Holt, 1971.
Curran, Eileen *Mountains and Volcanoes* Troll, 1985.
Dineen, Jacqueline *Let's Look At Rain* Brookwright, 1989.
Gans, Roma *Rock Collecting* Crowell, 1984.
Hopkins, Lee Bennett *The Sky Is Full of Song* Harper, 1983.
Johnson, Crockett *Will Spring Be Early? Or Will Spring Be Late?*
  Harper, 1990.
Keats, Ezra Jack *The Snowy Day* Puffin, 1976.

Lauber, Patricia *How We Learned the Earth Is Round* Harper, 1990.

Livingston, Myra Cohn *A Circle of Seasons* Holiday House, 1982.

McNulty, Faith *How to Dig a Hole to the Other Side of the World* Harper, 1979.

Milburn, Constance *Let's Look at the Seasons* Bookwright, 1988.

Orlowsky, Wallace and Thomas B. Perera
    Who Will Clean the Air? Coward McCann, 1971.
    Who Will Wash the River? Coward McCann, 1970

Palazzo, Janet *What Makes the Weather* Troll, 1982.

Prelutsky, Jack *It's Snowing! It's Snowing!* Greenwillow, 1984.

Pringle, Laurence *Twist, Wiggle, and Squirm: A Book About Earthworms* Crowell, 1973.

Quackenbush, Robert *Calling Dr. Quack* Lothrop, Lee, and Shepard, 1978.

Santrey, Laurence *What Makes the Wind?* Troll, 1982.

Simon, Seymour *Earth: Our Planet in Space* Four Winds, 1984.

Skofield, James *All Wet! All Wet!* Harper, 1984.

Stevens, Carla *Anna, Grandpa, and the Big Storm* Clarion, 1982.

Stolz, Mary *Storm in the Night* Harper, 1990.

Wandelmaier, Roy *Clouds* Troll, 1985.

Pages 68–93

Balestrino, Phillip *Hot as an Ice Cube* Crowell, 1971.

Berenstain, Stan and Jan *Bears on Wheels* Random House, 1969.

Berger, Melvin *Switch On, Switch Off* Harper, 1989.

Burningham, John *Mr. Gumpy's Motor Car* Holt, 1976.

Calhoun, Mary *Hot-Air Henry* Morrow, 1981.

Coerr, Eleanor *The Big Balloon Race* Harper, 1981.
    The Mixed-Up Mystery Smell Putnam, 1976.

Cole, Joanna *It's Too Noisy!* Crowell, 1989.

Couture, Susan Arkin *The Block Book* Harper, 1990.

Crews, Donald *Harbor* Greenwillow, 1982.

Ehlert, Lois *Color Farm* Harper, 1990.

Fleischman, Paul *Shadow Play* Harper, 1990.

Goffstein, Brooke *A House, A Home* Harper, 1989.

Holabird, Katharine *Angelina Ballerina* Crown, 1983.

Hopkins, Lee Bennett, ed. *Click, Rumble, Roar: Poems About Machines* Crowell, 1987.

Kirkpatrick, Rena K. *Look at Magnets* Raintree, 1985.

Kuskin, Karla *Roar and More* Harper, 1990.

Mahy, Margaret *The Boy with Two Shadows* Lippincott, 1988.

Marquardt, Max *Wilbur, Orville, and the Flying Machine* Raintree, 1989.

Scarry, Richard *Richard Scarry's Cars and Trucks and Things That Go* Western, 1974.

Seibert, Diane *Train Song* Harper, 1990.

Seixas, Judith S. *Water—What It Is, What It Does* Greenwillow, 1987.

Walsh, Ellen Stoll *Mouse Paint* Harcourt, 1989.

Westcott, Nadine Bernard *There's a Hole in the Bucket* Harper, 1990.